MODERN AND TRADITIONAL IRISH COOKING

MODERN AND TRADITIONAL ÍRÍSH COOKING

ETHEL MINOGUE

NEW BURLINGTON BOOKS

For Karim, Daragh, Shane and Peter
and with thanks to
Sam, and Tim and Zoe Hill

A QUINTET BOOK

Published by New Burlington Books
6 Blundell Street
London N7 9BH

ISBN 1-85348-103-3

This book was designed and produced by
Quintet Publishing Limited
6 Blundell Street
London N7 9BH

Creative Director: Peter Bridgewater
Art Director: Ian Hunt
Designer: Annie Moss
Editors: Judith Simons, Susie Ward,
Henrietta Wilkinson
Photographer: Tim Hill
Stylist: Zoe Hill
Ireland Photography: Trevor Wood, assisted by
Jonathan Higgins
Home Economist: Ethel Minogue

Typeset in Great Britain by
Context Typesetting, Brighton
Manufactured in Hong Kong by
Regent Publishing Services Limited
Printed in China

ADDITIONAL PICTURES
John Heseltine: page 52; Illustrated London News:
pages 47 *b*, 87 *b*; Irish Tourist Board: pages 14 *t*, 38/9,
43 *t*, Robert Opie Collection: pages 59 *r*, 99 *br*;
Trevor Wood and Michael Bull: pages 101 *b*, 115.

contents

Introduction 6

Soups 8

Starters and Egg Dishes 20

Fish and Shellfish 32

Meat Dishes 56

Poultry and Game 74

Vegetables and Salads 84

Desserts, Breads and Baking 96

Basic Recipes 120

Index 126

Introduction

TRADITIONAL IRISH FARE is famous for being simple and wholesome, and based as it is on some of the finest ingredients to be found in the world there is little need to dress it up with fancy sauces and dressings. Ireland is a land of plenty: its seas and rivers team with fish and seafood, such as salmon and trout, native oysters, lobsters, Dublin Bay prawns and giant scallops: the unpolluted pastures produce the finest beef, lamb and pork in the world; and the skies are full of game birds – pheasant, snipe, partridges and wild duck are everyday fare for many country people.

Irish cooking has a long history, and some of its traditions, such as the serving of boiled and roast meats on the same platter, date back to early Celtic times when the land was governed by a legal system called the Brehon Laws, which even laid down rules concerning food and hospitality. However, in more recent times, the increasing dependence of rural Ireland on the potato – a fickle crop at the best of times – compounded by cruel economic and social policies, lead to the terrible famines of the 1840s and '50s.

These tragedies virtually destroyed peasant cuisine. Dishes such as pork ciste, spiced beef and soda bread pre-date the famine, but many traditional dishes disappeared due to non-existent vegetable production. The author remembers a time when it was impossible to buy anything apart from potatoes, cabbage, carrots and onions in the west of Ireland and only recently have more 'exotic' foodstuffs like garlic, peppers, and kiwi fruit become available.

The traditional of Irish cooking continued in the more prosperous farmhouses and country estates, and this book is a collection of traditional recipes culled from old notebooks, Irish homes, hotels and restaurants. The author is also indebted to Monica Sheridan and Theodora Fitzgibbon, whose books and articles in *The Irish Times* have inspired many Irish cooks. Many of the modern recipes are a result of the author's experiments in a lighter style of cooking practised in her own restaurant. She has successfully dispelled the idea of Ireland as a culinary desert and believes in using traditional wholesome ingredients so that new dishes such as sea bass wrapped in seaweed, Cashel cheese and celery soup, scallops in champagne sauce and delicious and unusual salads are served along side traditional staples such as Brochan Roy, oatcakes and Irish stew.

A nation's diet is an important part of that country's history and culture. Irish food is very close to the earth and this book provides the best in both traditional and modern Irish cuisine to be heartily enjoyed with good wine and convivial conversation

SOUPS

Mutton Broth with Barley 11
Brotchan Roy 11
Pea and Ham Soup 12
White Onion Soup 13
Cashel Cheese and Celery Soup 15
Sorrel Soup 15
Leek and Mussel Soup 17
Fish Soup 18
Leek and Potato Soup 19

LEFT *Magnificent landscape, mountains and lakes – this is the very stuff of the countryside in the west of Ireland. This is the heartland of Irish traditional cooking, in which soups play a prominent part.*

Mutton Broth with Barley

COOKING TIME: 1 HOUR 20 MINUTES

INGREDIENTS

675 g/1½ lb neck of mutton on the bone
2 large onions, chopped
¼ cup/50 g/2 oz pearl barley
45 ml/3 tbsp soaked baricot (white) beans
7½ cups/1.75 L/3 pt brown stock (see Basic Recipes)
2 carrots, finely chopped
2 leeks, finely chopped
2 sticks of celery, finely chopped
2 white turnips, finely chopped
Salt and pepper
Chopped parsley

▲ Trim any fat off the neck meat. If you are using the leg of mutton, ask your butcher to bone and roll it for you.

▲ Put the meat in a large pan. Add the chopped onions, and the barley and beans. Simmer for an hour in the stock – skim, if necessary, and add all the vegetables. Continue to cook for about 20 minutes.

▲ Remove the bones before serving. Add salt and pepper to taste and garnish each bowl with chopped parsley.

Mutton broth used to be one of the staples in the Irish diet. Mutton is often difficult to get nowadays – the modern taste for young lamb has resulted in reduced quantities of mature meat in the marketplace. However, mutton is usually available in either Irish or Halal butcher's shops. If you are serving Mutton in Caper Sauce as the main course, the leg of mutton may be cooked in this broth; which is then served as the first course. Otherwise neck of mutton is excellent for soup.

Brotchan Roy

COOKING TIME: 40 MINUTES

INGREDIENTS

5 cups/1.1 L/2 pt chicken stock or milk (see Basic Recipes)
30 ml/2 tbsp medium oatmeal
6 young leeks
30 ml/2 tbsp butter
30 ml/2 tbsp chopped parsley
Salt and pepper
Pinch of mace
Cream and chopped chives to garnish

▲ Bring the chicken stock or milk to the boil. Sprinkle in the oatmeal, stirring all the time to prevent lumps.

▲ Cut the leeks – both white and green parts – into ½-in/1-cm lengths. Wash them well and soften in the butter. Add the leeks to the simmering oatmeal mixture.

▲ Cook for about 15 minutes. Add the chopped parsley, salt, pepper and mace.

▲ Serve in warm bowls, with a swirl of cream and chopped chives. Hot buttered oatcakes (*see* Oatcakes) are delicious with this soup.

LEFT *The Irish are a race of farmers. County Donegal is famous sheep country and the mutton produced there is a basis for many soups and broths.*

Dried peas are a very popular vegetable in rural Ireland – until recently, except in the larger towns, it was almost impossible to buy any fresh vegetables apart from potatoes, onions, cabbage and carrots.
I felt quite shocked last year being able to buy peppers and kiwi fruit in a small village in West Clare.
Dried whole peas, marrow fats, or split green peas may be used for this soup. Yellow peas may also be used and taste just as good, but the green colour is more appealing with the ham.

Pea and Ham Soup

COOKING TIME: 2 HOURS OR MORE

INGREDIENTS

2 large onions
30 ml/2 tbsp bacon fat
1 ham bone and trimmings or 2 knuckles of bacon
450 g/1 lb dried peas (soaked for at least 3 hours)
1 bunch of fresh herbs
1 bay leaf
3¾-5 Am pt/1.75-2.25 L/3-4 pt bacon stock or water used for boiling ham
Salt and pepper
Chopped mint and parsley

▲ Soften the onions in the bacon fat. Put them in a large pan with the ham bone or knuckles and add the soaked peas, the bunch of herbs and bay leaf. Cover these with the stock or ham water. Bring the broth slowly to the boil, then simmer for 2 hours.

▲ Take out the bones – dice any ham or bacon trimmings, which can go back into the soup.

▲ If the soup is too thick, water or milk may be added to thin it. If you add milk, bring the soup to simmering point, but do not boil it.

▲ Season and serve with chopped mint and parsley. Small pieces of bacon are a nice addition.

White Onion Soup

COOKING TIME: 1 HOUR

This soup is a nice change from the French brown onion version. This is Theodora Fitzgibbons' recipe; like her, I remember onion soup being a cure-all in the same league as hot whiskey.

INGREDIENTS

70 ml/4 heaped tbsp butter
450 g/1 lb onions, thinly sliced
2 cloves
35 ml/2 heaped tbsp plain (all-purpose) flour
Pinch of powdered mace or nutmeg
1 bay leaf
4 cups/900 ml/$1\frac{1}{2}$ pt chicken or pork stock (see Basic Recipes)
$1\frac{1}{4}$ cups/300 ml/$\frac{1}{2}$ pt milk
Salt and pepper
$\frac{2}{3}$ cup/150 ml/$\frac{1}{4}$ pt cream or 15-45 ml/1-3 tbsp grated hard cheese

▲ Heat the butter and, when foaming, add the onions and the cloves. Let the onions soften, but not change colour.

▲ Sprinkle over the flour – mix well and cook, stirring constantly for 1 minute. Then add the mace or nutmeg, the bay leaf and the stock. Stir all the time, until it boils and you can see that it is smooth.

▲ Simmer until the onions are well-cooked, then gradually add the milk. Stir continuously and, when it boils, remove the cloves and bay leaf.

▲ This soup may be liquidized, but is much nicer served as is with the addition of the cream or grated cheese.

IRISH STORES

Links between town and country have always been finely balanced in Ireland. Many of the stores are full of native products and many of the Irish still prefer the traditional cooking of their ancestors to modern convenience food.

LEFT *The imposing Rock of Cashel, crowned by its 13th-century cathedral, dominates this part of County Tipperary. The local cheese is equally celebrated.*

Sorrel Soup

COOKING TIME: 30 MINUTES

INGREDIENTS

60 ml/4 tbsp butter
1 large Spanish onion
4 cloves of garlic
450 g/1 lb sorrel
10 cups/2.25 L/4 pt chicken stock (see Basic Recipes)
30 ml/2 tbsp medium oatmeal
Salt and pepper
2/3 cup/150 ml/1/4 pt lightly whipped cream

▲ Melt the butter. Chop the onion and the garlic and soften them in the butter. Wash and tear the sorrel, and melt it in the butter and onions. Add the stock and bring to the boil.

▲ Scatter in the oatmeal and stir until cooked. Season the soup to taste and simmer for about an hour.

▲ Serve in warm bowls with a dollop of whipped cream.

Cashel Cheese and Celery Soup

COOKING TIME: 45 MINUTES

INGREDIENTS

3 large onions
1 head of celery
60 ml/4 tbsp butter
2 cloves of garlic
5-7 1/2 cups/1.1-1.75 L/2-3 pt chicken or vegetable stock (see Basic Recipes)
100 g/1/4 lb Cashel blue cheese (other cow's blue cheese will do)
A little cream to blend with the cheese
Cubes of bread fried in olive oil or bacon fat and drained (croutons)

▲ Slice the onions and chop the celery. Soften them in the butter. Add the cloves of garlic and the stock and simmer for about 40 minutes – or until the onions and celery are cooked.

▲ Blend the blue cheese and cream together and stir into the soup just before serving. Season to taste and serve in large warm bowls with croutons.

INGREDIENTS

5 Am pt/2.25 L/4 pt mussels
4 leeks
2 shallots
2 cloves of garlic
45 ml/3 tbsp chopped parsley
15 ml/1 tbsp chopped dill
15 ml/1 tbsp chopped chives
Half bottle dry white wine
100g /4 oz butter, cut into small cubes
5 cups/1.1 L/2 pt fish stock (see *Basic Recipes)*
Small pinch of saffron soaked in water
Black pepper

Leek and Mussel Soup

COOKING TIME: 40-50 MINUTES

▲ Prepare the mussels by removing the beards and any barnacles. Scrub well and rinse in clean water. Throw away any mussels that remain open when tapped – any mussels that feel very heavy will be full of mud and must be discarded as well.

▲ Chop the leeks, shallots and garlic finely. Put in a long pan with the parsley, dill and chives. Pour the wine over the clean mussels. Place on a high heat until the mussels are steamed open. Discard any mussels that remain firmly closed.

▲ Take out the mussels, shell, and put aside. Reserve all the delicious liquor in the pan.

▲ Whip the butter cubes into the liquor and add the fish stock to the pan. Stir in the soaked saffron strands, simmer gently over a low heat for a few minutes, and season with black pepper.

▲ Add the shelled mussels and heat in the liquor but do not boil, as the mussels will get leathery.

▲ Serve the soup in warm bowls garnished with more chopped chives and parsley. Pass slices of soda bread (*see* Brown Soda Bread).

LEFT *Ireland's bountiful coasts have always been a rich source of sea food. When it comes to soups, mussels are still a traditional favourite.*

Fish Soup

COOKING TIME: 30 MINUTES

INGREDIENTS

450-675 g/1-1½ lb mixed vegetables, finely chopped (carrots, shallots, onions, fennel, leeks, celery, tomatoes, potatoes)

60 ml/4 tbsp butter

5 cups/1.1 L/2 pt fish stock (see *Basic Recipes)*

Bay leaf and fresh herbs

2 cloves of garlic

675-900 g/1½-2 lb firm white fish

1 glass dry white wine

30 ml/2 tbsp chopped parsley

⅔ cup/150 ml/¼ pt cream

Salt, pepper and paprika

▲ Toss the vegetables in 30 ml/2 tbsp butter. Add the stock, herbs and garlic, and simmer until the vegetables are cooked.

▲ Cut the fish into chunks and poach gently in the wine. Remove the fish from the liquid, whisk in the remaining butter and add to the stock and vegetables. Sprinkle in the chopped parsley, flake the fish and add to the soup.

▲ Just before serving, add the cream and heat to just below boiling point. Do not boil. Season, and add a pinch of paprika in the bowls.

▲ This fish soup is very good served with croutons and garlic mayonnaise (*see* Basic Recipes), and may be made with either smoked cod or haddock. For another variation, add a pinch of curry powder instead of the paprika at the end.

INGREDIENTS

450 g/1 lb leeks
450 g/1 lb floury potatoes
60 ml/2 tbsp butter
5 cups/1.1 L/2 pt chicken or ham stock (see Basic Recipes)
Large bunch of herbs, including some celery tops
Salt and pepper
Cubes of bread fried in olive oil or bacon fat and drained (croutons)
Cream

Leek and Potato Soup

COOKING TIME: 50-60 MINUTES

▲ Cut up and wash the leeks; peel and chop the potatoes. Melt the butter and soften the leeks in a pan. Add the potatoes and cook gently (do not fry) for about 10 minutes. Add the stock and bunch of herbs.
▲ Season to taste and simmer for about an hour.
▲ Add the fried croutons to the soup with a little cream when serving.

starters and egg dishes

Wild Mushroom Omelette 22

Wicklow Pancakes 23

Soft-boiled Eggs in Ramekins with Onion Sauce 24

Chicken Livers with Marsala 24

Black Pudding with Apple Purée 26

Fish Creams 27

Smoked Salmon Stuffed Tomatoes 28

Scrambled Eggs with Smoked Salmon 29

Sweetbreads with Bacon 30

Buttermilk Pancakes 30

Chicken, Apple and Black Pudding Filling 30

Spinach and Chopped Egg Filling 31

LEFT *A typical Connemara landscape, with mountains sheltering rich fields. In the Irish countryside, you will find all sorts of foods growing in the wild, many of which are used in traditional Irish starters.*

Any edible wild mushrooms may be used for this. But be very careful if you are a novice mushroom hunter. Delicious as this is, you do not want to make it your last meal on earth.

Wild Mushroom Omelette

COOKING TIME: 10 MINUTES

INGREDIENTS

450 g/1 lb chanterelle mushrooms
6 fresh eggs
15 ml/1 tbsp chopped fresh herbs
Salt and pepper
45 ml/3 tbsp olive oil

▲ Beat the eggs with the herbs and salt and pepper. Slice the chanterelles.

▲ Put the olive oil in a non-stick skillet or pan. Cook the chanterelles for about five minutes, then add the egg mixture. Cook over a moderate heat until almost set. Fold and serve immediately.

RIGHT *Powerscourt, County Wicklow, Ireland has a country-house cooking tradition dating back to the days of the British Ascendancy, which has deeply influenced culinary style.*

Wicklow Pancakes

PREPARATION AND COOKING TIME:
10-15 MINUTES + 30 MINUTES

INGREDIENTS

450 g/1 lb onions
675 g/1½ lb potatoes, sliced
90 ml/6 tbsp olive oil
Salt and black pepper
6 eggs
Parsley

▲ Peel and slice the onions and potatoes and stew in the olive oil until they are very well cooked – do try not to brown either the onions or the potatoes. Drain off the excess oil, season to taste.

▲ Whisk the eggs in a large bowl, then add the potato and onion mixture, along with some chopped parsley. Put a little oil in a pan and pour some of the mixture in until it is nearly 1 in/2.5 cm thick.

▲ Cook over a moderate heat until reasonably firm, then turn over with the help of a dinner plate. Cook for a few minutes and turn out.

▲ Cut into wedges and eat hot or cold.

Chicken Livers with Marsala

Soft-Boiled Eggs in Ramekins with Onion Sauce

COOKING TIME: 25 MINUTES

INGREDIENTS

2 soft-boiled eggs per person
3 large Spanish onions
60 ml/4 tbsp butter or olive oil
A little cream, béchamel sauce, or crème fraîche

▲ Put the eggs in boiling water for exactly 4 minutes. Then plunge them into cold water. When they are cool enough to handle, tap them all over with a spoon – don't bash them too hard or you will have a handful of soft-boiled egg. Peel the eggs carefully and place two per person in each ramekin.

▲ Thinly slice the onions and cook slowly in the butter or olive oil for at least 20 minutes. The onions must be very well-cooked, but not too brown. They may then be mixed with a little cream, béchamel sauce (*see* Sauces) or crème fraîche.

▲ Put a few spoonfuls of the creamy onions on top of the eggs and warm the ramekins in the oven for 5 minutes. Finish under a grill, until the sauce bubbles.

▲ There are delicious ways of varying this using tomato sauce, cheese sauce (*see* Basic Recipes), or sorrel sauce (*see* Poached Salmon with Sorrel Sauce).

Chicken Livers with Marsala

COOKING TIME: ABOUT 10 MINUTES

INGREDIENTS

60 ml/4 tbsp butter
½ Spanish onion, finely chopped
3 large cloves of garlic
450 g/1 lb fresh chicken livers, cleaned and trimmed
Chopped herbs
1 glass Marsala
4 hard-boiled egg yolks, finely chopped or pressed through a sieve (strainer)
Brown toast, buttered

▲ Melt the butter in a heavy pan. Soften the onion and garlic in it. Add the trimmed livers and sauté until they are lightly cooked. Add the chopped herbs and cook for another few minutes.

▲ Pour in the Marsala and turn up the heat for about 2 minutes. Scrape into a bowl and chop roughly. Add the finely chopped or sieved egg yolks and pile onto triangles of buttered toast to serve. This dish is delicious hot or cold.

Soft-Boiled Eggs in Ramekins

Life in the country cottage revolves around its kitchen, where the entire household gathers to prepare and enjoy meals.

Black Pudding with Apple Purée

COOKING TIME: 5 HOURS

INGREDIENTS

225 g/½ lb pig's liver
675 g/1½ lb chopped, unrendered lard
15 cups/3.5 L/3 qt pig's blood
450 g/1 lb fresh breadcrumbs
2½ cups/600 ml/1 pt water from cooking the liver
1 cup medium oatmeal
1 onion, chopped
2.5 ml/½ tsp allspice
5 ml/1 tsp each rubbed sage and thyme
Salt and pepper to taste

▲ Gently poach the liver in boiling salted water. Drain and reserve the water. Roughly chop the liver into a large bowl. Add the lard and all the other ingredients and stir very well.

▲ Pack the mixture into oiled pudding basins. Cover with greaseproof (waxed) paper and foil. Tie securely and steam for 4-5 hours. Unmould and leave until cold.

▲ Cut into slices and fry in bacon fat or lard, until crisp on both sides. Serve with grilled (broiled) tomatoes and apple purée.

Apple Purée

COOKING TIME: 20 MINUTES

INGREDIENTS

900 g/2 lb tart cooking apples
15 ml/1 tbsp brown sugar
Chopped fresh sage

▲ Peel and core the apples. Stew with the brown sugar until soft.

▲ Mash with a fork and add a touch of chopped sage. Serve hot with the black pudding.

▲ Note: Slices of commercially made black pudding sausage may be used. Try to buy it from a reputable butcher, as the supermarket version is not worth eating. If you want to be really indulgent, eat it with fried soda bread.

INGREDIENTS

450 g/1 lb smoked haddock
2 cups/100g/¼ lb fresh breadcrumbs
Salt and pepper
½ cup/100 g/¼ lb unsalted butter, melted
2 eggs, beaten
2½ cups/600 ml/1 pt béchamel sauce (see Basic Recipes)
30 ml/2 tbsp chopped parsley
Grated nutmeg

Fish Creams

COOKING TIME: 1 HOUR 20 MINUTES

▲ Lightly poach the smoked haddock. Remove the skin and bones and flake and mash the fish. Add the breadcrumbs and seasoning. Mix in the melted butter and beaten eggs. Pour into a pudding basin or 4-6 ramekins.

▲ Cover with greaseproof (waxed) paper or foil, and steam over boiling water for an hour – less if you use the ramekins.

▲ Meanwhile, make a béchamel sauce and stir in the chopped parsley and grated nutmeg to taste.

▲ When the fish creams are cooked, unmould into a warmed serving dish and pour the sauce over them. Serve hot.

▲ Note: Vary the sauce by using cheese, or cooked onions, or mushrooms, instead of the parsley.

Smoked Salmon Stuffed Tomatoes

COOKING TIME: 20 MINUTES

▲ Preheat the oven. Cut the tops off the tomatoes. Scoop out the insides, throw away the husks and place the tomato pulp in a bowl. Chop the shallots and the onion finely and mix with the tomato pulp.

▲ Purée the smoked salmon and add to the bowl. Chop the dill finely, place in the bowl with the smoked salmon and all the remaining ingredients. Mix well.

▲ Spoon the mixture back into the tomatoes, put the tomato lids on and bake for about 20 minutes.

▲ Serve on a bed of watercress. These stuffed tomatoes are good hot or cold.

INGREDIENTS

8 medium-sized tomatoes
225 g/½ lb smoked salmon offcuts
2 shallots
1 Spanish onion
Bunch of dill
2 cups/100g/4 oz fresh breadcrumbs
1 lemon
15 ml/1 tbsp cream or curd cheese
Tabasco
Bunch of watercress

OVEN TEMPERATURE:
180°C/350°F/GAS MARK 4

Scrambled Eggs with Smoked Salmon

COOKING TIME: 15 MINUTES

INGREDIENTS

2 eggs per person
15 ml/1 tbsp milk per person
Knob of butter
1 slice smoked salmon per person (or some trimmings)
1 slice buttered brown toast per person
Chopped dill or parsley
Black pepper
1 lemon

▲ Beat the eggs and milk until well blended but not frothy.

▲ Melt the butter over a low heat. Add the eggs and milk and cook gently, adding the chopped salmon just before the eggs are ready. (Scrambled eggs should always be taken off the heat while the eggs are still very moist as they will continue to cook in their own heat.)

▲ Pile the egg and salmon mixture on the hot buttered brown toast, garnish with chopped dill or parsley, season with freshly ground pepper and top with a lemon wedge.

Buttermilk Pancakes

INGREDIENTS

Good ¾ cup/100 g/¼ lb wholemeal flour

Pinch of salt

1 egg

⅔ cup/150 ml/¼ pt buttermilk

30 ml/2 tbsp butter

▲ Mix the flour and salt; make a well in the middle. Stir in the egg and buttermilk, but do not beat too much at this stage. Melt the butter and beat into the mixture with a wooden spoon. Let stand for at least half an hour before using.

▲ Place a small ladle of batter on a crêpe pan, and shake the pan so the batter spreads evenly. When little holes appear on the pancake, it is ready to turn over. Do so.

▲ These pancakes are very light and may be kept warm in the oven until needed.

▲ Keep warm between two plates until they are ready to be filled.

Sweetbreads with Bacon

PREPARATION TIME: 3 HOURS

INGREDIENTS

900 g/2 lb sweetbreads, skinned and trimmed

A little plain (all-purpose) flour

1 egg, beaten

60 ml/4 tbsp butter

100 g/¼ lb button mushrooms

2 cloves of garlic

175 g/6 oz rindless streaky bacon, cut into 1-inch/2.5-cm pieces

15 ml/1 tbsp Madeira

15 ml/1 tbsp cream

Chopped parsley and chives

Black pepper

▲ Soak the sweetbreads in cold salted water for at least three hours. Blanch in fresh boiling water for 5-6 minutes. Drain and plunge into cold water. Cut off the gristly bits and the skin.

▲ Dip the sweetbreads in beaten egg and flour. Fry in butter for a few minutes and keep warm.

▲ Sauté the garlic, mushrooms and bacon in the butter. Stir in the Madeira and cream. Bubble for a few minutes. Add the sweetbreads, parsley, chives and some black pepper.

▲ Serve on toast or fried bread as an hors d'oeuvre, or with rice.

Chicken, Apple and Black Pudding Filling

COOKING TIME: 15-20 MINUTES

INGREDIENTS

4 shallots

2 eating apples

1 large tart cooking apple

30 ml/2 tbsp butter

175 g/6 oz black pudding

175 g/6 oz cooked chicken (a good way to use up leftover chicken)

▲ Chop the shallots, peel and chop the apples, and cook in the butter until the cooking apple is mushy.

▲ Peel and cube the black pudding and chop the chicken. Add both to the apple sauce.

▲ Heat through, and fill the pancakes.

INGREDIENTS

1 onion
30 ml/2 tbsp butter
450 g/1 lb spinach, washed
1¼ cups/300 ml/½ pt béchamel sauce (see Basic Recipes)
4 hard-boiled eggs, chopped
Chopped parsley and dill
Grated nutmeg

Spinach and Chopped Egg Filling

COOKING TIME: 30 MINUTES

▲ Chop the onion and soften in the butter. Add the spinach and cook until soft and reduced to half its bulk.
▲ When the spinach is tender, add the béchamel sauce.
▲ Fold in the chopped hard-boiled egg, parsley, dill and grated nutmeg.
▲ Note: Buttermilk pancakes are also very good with Scrambled Eggs with Smoked Salmon as a filling (*see* recipe of that name). Also try cooked ham with onion and parsley sauce (*see* Basic Recipes).

The south of Ireland's Catholic tradition is an integral part of the Irish heritage. This, too, has influenced Irish cookery, with the ritual of feast and fast days.

Fish and Shellfish

Griddled Salmon Steaks with Herb Butter 34
Baked Stuffed Salmon with Cucumber Sauce 35
Poached Salmon with Sorrel Sauce 36
Baked Stuffed Trout 37
Scallops in Champagne Sauce 38
Scallops Served on the Shell with Mushrooms and Duchesse Potatoes 39
Mussel and Onion Stew 40
Stuffed Mussels 41
Fried Oysters 42
Oysters in Champagne Sauce 42
Angels on Horseback 43
Cod Baked with Bacon 45
Fish Steaks with Mussels 45
Smoked Fish Pie 46
Sea Bass Cooked with Seaweed in a Paper Case 47
Ray with Brown Butter Sauce 48
Plaice (Flounder) with Mustard Sauce 48
Dublin Lawyer 50
Dublin Bay Prawns in Garlic Butter 51
Devilled Crab 53
Creamed Crab 53
Kedgeree 54
Soused Herrings with Sour Cream 55

LEFT *Towering cliffs dominate this seascape near Portrush, in the north. Fishing is one of Ireland's key industries and the foods that come from the sea are culinary staples.*

INGREDIENTS

4 fresh salmon steaks (about 175 g/6 oz each)

½ cup/100 g/4 oz butter

15 ml/1 tbsp chopped parsley

15 ml/1 tbsp tarragon and chives, chopped

Griddled Salmon Steaks with Herb Butter

COOKING TIME: 8 MINUTES

▲ Lightly oil a griddle or a heavy pan. Place a salmon steak on the hot griddle and cook for about 4 minutes on each side.

▲ Work the butter, the parsley and the tarragon and chives together until you have a herb butter. Serve on hot plates with knobs of butter on top of the steaks.

▲ Salmon steaks make a quick and delicious meal served with minted new potatoes and green beans.

▲ Note on herb butters: When fresh herbs are in season, it is a good idea to have a session of making different varieties. Herb and garlic butters may be kept in a roll shape in foil and frozen until needed. Soften unsalted butter and work in the chopped herbs:

Dill, parsley, lemon and tarragon butters are good with fish.
Tarragon, garlic and basil butter are delicious with chicken.
Thyme and rosemary butters are particularly good with lamb.

The rivers and lakes of the west are an ideal home for the princely salmon – hard to catch, but delicious to eat.

INGREDIENTS

1 salmon, about 1.75 kg/4 lb in weight
⅔ cup/150 ml/¼ pt dry white wine
3 cups/175 g/6 oz fresh breadcrumbs
15 ml/1 tbsp chopped parsley
Zest of one lemon
50 g/2 oz mushrooms, finely chopped
2 hard-boiled eggs, chopped
Butter, melted

Baked Stuffed Salmon with Cucumber Sauce

COOKING TIME: 1 HOUR

▲ Preheat the oven. Clean and descale the salmon. Make the stuffing by mixing all the other ingredients except the wine in a bowl. Then put the stuffing inside the fish.

▲ Place the fish in a buttered baking dish. Pour the wine over it and cover with foil. Bake for 15 minutes to the pound. Baste occasionally.

▲ When cooked, remove the skin and small side bones and fins – keep hot.

▲ To make the sauce, cook the cucumber in the liquor from the baking pan on a high heat. Then beat in the butter cubes gradually. When the sauce looks thick, pour over the salmon.

FOR THE CUCUMBER SAUCE:

1 cucumber, peeled, seeded and chopped
1¼ cups/300 ml/½ pt liquor from cooking the fish
60 ml/4 tbsp unsalted (sweet) butter, cut into cubes

OVEN TEMPERATURE:
180°C/350°F/GAS MARK 4

Poached Salmon with Sorrel Sauce

COOKING TIME: 8-10 MINUTES

INGREDIENTS

Allow one cutlet of salmon (wild preferably) per person

FOR THE SORREL SAUCE:

½ cup/100 g/¼ lb unsalted (sweet) butter

1 large bunch of sorrel, washed and chopped

1¼ cups/300 ml/½ pt double (heavy) cream or crème fraîche

Salt and pepper

▲ Poach the salmon in boiling salted water for about 8 minutes. Remove and keep on a warm plate.

▲ Melt the butter in a saucepan. Add the chopped sorrel – it melts into the butter very quickly. When it has bubbled for a few minutes, add the cream and seasoning, bring to the boil and simmer for 10 minutes. If you are using crème fraîche, boil very rapidly for a few minutes.

▲ Pour the sauce over the poached salmon and serve immediately.

INGREDIENTS

4 one-portion-sized trout
1 cup/50 g/2 oz fresh white breadcrumbs
1 onion, finely chopped
Knob of butter
2 hard-boiled eggs, finely chopped
Lemon zest
4 small mushrooms, chopped
Tabasco
Chopped parsley
Salt and pepper
A little milk
White or red wine

OVEN TEMPERATURE:
180°C/350°F/GAS MARK 4

Baked Stuffed Trout

COOKING TIME: ABOUT 20 MINUTES

▲ Preheat the oven. Clean the trout and pat them dry inside and out. Keep them in a cold place while you make the stuffing.
▲ Put the fresh breadcrumbs in a bowl. Soften the onion in a little butter over a low heat and add to the breadcrumbs, together with the lemon zest, finely chopped hard-boiled eggs, chopped mushrooms, Tabasco, parsley and seasoning to taste. Moisten with a little milk until the stuffing holds together.
▲ Stuff each trout with the mixture. Splash with a little wine and then wrap in foil, or greaseproof (waxed) paper. Cook in a moderate oven for about 20 minutes, or until the fish feels firm.
▲ Serve with parsley sauce (*see* Basic Recipes).

Trout, too, team in Irish rivers and the cooking method described here is ideally suited to preserving the fresh flavour of the fish.

INGREDIENTS

8 large scallops (on the shell, if possible)
4 spring (green) onions
Chopped root ginger to taste
2 cloves of garlic
60 ml/4 tbsp butter, melted
1 glass champagne
Chopped flat-leaf parsley

Scallops in Champagne Sauce

COOKING TIME: 15 MINUTES

▲ Remove the scallops from the shell, using a short bladed knife. Discard the black bits and keep the white flesh and the coral. Keep any liquor from the shell and reserve the shells.

▲ Slice the spring onions, ginger and garlic. Fry for a few minutes in the melted butter, then add the sliced scallops and their liquor. Toss the shellfish and onion mixture over a high heat for about 5 minutes. Remove the large pieces from the pan with a slotted spoon and keep warm.

▲ Pour the glass of champagne into the juices in the pan. Cook on a high heat until the sauce is reduced. Serve the chopped scallops on the deep half shell with the sauce. Garnish with the chopped parsley.

This may sound rather extravagant, but it requires very little champagne. It is also no hardship to drink the rest of the bottle while eating the scallops!

Ireland's scallop beds are justly famous and scallops fresh from the sea can be bought in many coastal-town markets, such as Ballybunion.

Scallops Served on the Shell with Mushrooms and Duchesse Potatoes

COOKING TIME: 30-40 MINUTES

▲ Wash and clean the scallops. Poach for 5 minutes on top of the stove in a court bouillon made with the water, wine, herbs, onion, salt and pepper.

▲ Drain the scallops, reserving the court bouillon, and slice them. Slice the mushrooms. Melt about 60 ml/4 tbsp of butter in a pan and toss the mushrooms and scallops in it for a few minutes. Keep warm in a covered dish.

▲ In a saucepan, melt ½ cup/100g/1¼ lb of butter and add the flour. Make a roux and cook for a few minutes. Cool the roux a little, then strain the reserved court bouillon and add to the roux very gradually. Stir with a whisk to prevent lumps. Bring to the boil, stirring with a whisk, and boil for 2 minutes.

▲ Take the sauce off the heat and thicken with two egg yolks, beaten with some of the court bouillon. Heat to simmering point, but do not boil, or the eggs will cook and go lumpy. Whisk 60 ml/4 tbsp of butter into the sauce and season to taste.

▲ Preheat the oven. Clean the scallop shells. Put a spoonful of sauce on each shell. Top with the scallops and mushrooms with 2 bits of coral on each shell. Cover with more sauce and scatter breadcrumbs on top.

▲ Pipe some mashed potato around the edge of the shell and brown in a very hot oven. Serve immediately.

INGREDIENTS

12 scallops, and 6 shells
1¼ cups/300 ml/½ pt water
1 glass dry white wine
Bunch of sweet herbs
Bay leaves
1 onion
Salt and freshly ground white pepper
1 cup/225 g/½ lb unsalted butter
225 g/½ lb button mushrooms
15 ml/1 tbsp flour
2 egg yolks
Breadcrumbs
450 g/1 lb well-flavoured mashed potatoes

OVEN TEMPERATURE:
180°C/350°F/GAS MARK 4

INGREDIENTS

5 Am pt/2.25 L/4 pt mussels
⅔ cup/150 ml/¼ pt dry white wine and water, mixed
6 Spanish onions, sliced
60 ml/4 tbsp butter or olive oil
4 shallots, chopped
6 cloves of garlic
2 carrots, chopped
4 potatoes
1 bouquet garni
Chopped parsley
Black pepper

Mussel and Onion Stew

COOKING TIME: 80 MINUTES

▲ Scrub and debeard the mussels. Place them in a large saucepan with the white wine and some water. Cook on a high heat until the mussels are open – remember to discard any that remain firmly shut. Remove the mussels and strain the liquor.

▲ In another pan, soften the onions in butter or olive oil. Add the shallots, garlic and chopped carrots. Peel and slice the potatoes, put them in the pan with the bouquet garni, parsley and the liquor from cooking the mussels. Season to taste with pepper. Simmer for about an hour.

▲ Meanwhile, shell the mussels and reserve.

▲ Take a ladle full of the vegetable broth from the pot, making sure you include some potatoes, and liquidize. Add to the rest of the vegetables again and put all the mussels into the pot. Simmer until the mussels are hot. (Do not boil as the mussels will get tough.)

▲ Serve in deep bowls with wedges of garlic bread.

Stuffed Mussels

COOKING TIME: 20 MINUTES

INGREDIENTS

48 large mussels
White wine
1 cup/225 g/½ lb unsalted butter
10 cloves of garlic, crushed
2 cups/100 g/¼ lb breadcrumbs
Lemon wedges

▲ Debeard and scrub the mussels. Throw away any mussels that remain open when tapped. Steam open the mussels in a little white wine and water. Drain and take off the top shell.

▲ Soften the butter a little with your hands. Add the crushed garlic cloves and work the breadcrumbs into the garlic butter.

▲ Put a knob of the stuffing on each mussel and place under a hot grill (broiler).

▲ Serve very hot with lemon wedges and crusty French bread.

Oysters in Champagne Sauce

Fried Oysters

INGREDIENTS

20 oysters

BATTER:

good 3/4 cup/100 g/4 oz flour

Salt and pepper

Pinch of cayenne pepper

1 egg

2/3 cup/150 ml/1/4 pt milk

Oil for frying

Lemon wedges

▲ Mix the dry ingredients in a bowl. Make a well in the middle and mix in the egg and the milk, making a smooth batter. Leave for 30 minutes.

▲ Open the oysters, dip them in the batter, and fry in hot oil. Drain on kitchen towels. Serve hot with lemon wedges.

Oysters in Champagne Sauce

COOKING TIME: 20 MINUTES

INGREDIENTS

2/3 cup/150 ml/1/4 pt Hollandaise sauce (see Basic Recipes)

2 shallots, finely chopped

1 glass champagne

16 oysters on the half shell

▲ Make the Hollandaise sauce (*see* Basic Recipes). Add some finely chopped shallots and the glass of champagne to the sauce.

▲ Spoon a little of the sauce on each oyster, bubble under the grill (broiler) for less than 2 minutes and serve.

Fresh oysters from Ireland's coasts, such as those from Tralee Bay in County Kerry, can simply be eaten raw, with a touch of lemon and accompanied by Ireland's equally celebrated beer – Guinness.

The best oysters in Ireland come from Galway, where every September there is a great oyster festival. It is really a sacrilege to cook such oysters. They are best eaten on the half shell, served on a bed of crushed ice and seaweed, with a lemon wedge and fresh brown bread and butter.
Recently, the Portuguese type, or rock oysters, have been cultivated on the northwest coast of Ireland. They do not have a 'season', like the Galway oysters, and do not have such a sweet taste. However, when they are very fresh they really taste of the sea. They tend to be cheaper than the natives, so it is more feasible to use them for cooking.
In the United States, there is yet another variety with a rough shell like the Portuguese oyster.

Angels on Horseback

COOKING TIME: 10 MINUTES

▲ Open the oysters and take out the flesh. Roll one strip of bacon around each oyster. Secure with a cocktail stick.
▲ Cook under a hot grill (broiler) and serve on hot triangles of fried bread.

INGREDIENTS

12 oysters
12 strips of rindless fatty bacon
12 cocktail sticks
12 triangles of fried bread

Wherever you go on the Irish coast, you will find fishermen, fishing boats, the opportunity to try your skills at sea fishing and the reward of eating your catch.

Fish Steaks with Mussels

Cod Baked with Bacon

COOKING TIME: 65 MINUTES

INGREDIENTS

1 Spanish onion, sliced
90 ml/6 tbsp butter
450 g/1 lb potatoes, parboiled and thinly sliced
Salt and pepper
4 good-sized cod steaks, or firm white fish steaks of your choice
225 g/½ lb lean smoked streaky bacon
1¼ cups/300 ml/½ pt cream or milk
Chopped parsley

OVEN TEMPERATURE:
180°C/350°F/GAS MARK 4

▲ Preheat the oven. Soften the onion in 60 ml/4 tbsp butter and place some of it in the bottom of a baking dish. Put the sliced potato on top and season. Put the cod steaks on top of the potatoes and cover with the rest of the onions and the bacon.

▲ Place in the oven. After 15 minutes pour the cream into the dish, dot with 30 ml/2 tbsp butter and replace in the oven for another 40 minutes.

▲ Cover with parsley and serve with Potato Cakes (*see* recipe) and a green salad. This dish is also good cooked without the cream, but it must be covered with foil from the beginning of the cooking.

Cod Baked with Bacon

Fish Steaks with Mussels

COOKING TIME: 30 MINUTES

INGREDIENTS

4 large firm, white fish steaks
Seasoned flour
⅔ cup/150 ml/5 fl oz virgin olive oil
900 g/2 lb ripe tomatoes (or 2 cans chopped tomatoes)
1 large Spanish onion
4 large cloves of garlic
½ cup/100 g/¼ lb unsalted butter, cut into cubes
1 glass dry white wine
2¼ cups/600 ml/1 pt mussels, cleaned and debearded
225 g/½ lb rice, cooked 'al dente'
Chopped parsley

▲ Dip the fish steaks in seasoned flour and fry them in 30 ml/2 tbsp of olive oil. Keep warm.

▲ Skin and chop the tomatoes. Chop the onion and the garlic and cook in the remainder of the olive oil and 60 ml/4 tbsp of butter. Then add the white wine and simmer for a while.

▲ Add the cleaned mussels and cover with a lid. Cook over a high heat until the mussels have opened. Shake the pan from time to time during the cooking. Take off the flame and remove the mussels and keep with the fish. Put the pan back on the heat and reduce the sauce a little.

▲ Add the rest of the butter cubes and whisk until melted, then add the cooked rice and heat through. Shake the pan again while heating.

▲ Put the fish steaks on a serving dish and cover with the mixture. Arrange the mussels in their shells on top and garnish with chopped parsley.

FOOD FROM THE SEA

No part of Ireland is more than 60 miles from the sea and consequently fish and other sea foods are very much part of the Irish culinary tradition. On many a country inn counter, you will find a saucer of some variety of seaweed put there for you to chew on, while, on the coast itself – especially in Donegal – modern fishing has meant a new level of prosperity. A walk around the harbour at Killybegs, Ireland's premier fishing port, shows you exactly how life has changed, with huge deep-sea trawlers lining up with small inshore boats to roam the seas from Donegal Bay to Norway.

Smoked Fish Pie

COOKING TIME: 20 MINUTES

INGREDIENTS

2½ cups/600 ml/1 pt béchamel sauce (see Basic Recipes)

1 glass dry white wine

30 ml/2 tbsp cream

350 g/¾ lb smoked haddock or finan haddie, cooked, boned and skinned (other firm-fleshed, smoked fish can be used)

175 g/6 oz prawn (shrimp) tails, cooked

100 g/4 oz cooked button mushrooms

15 ml/1 tbsp chopped chives and parsley

350 ml/¾ lb flaky or puff pastry (see Basic Recipes)

Milk or egg, to glaze

OVEN TEMPERATURE:
220°C-230°C/
425°F-450°F/GAS MARK 7-8

▲ Preheat the oven. In a bowl, pour in the béchamel sauce. Add the wine and cream, then mix in all the other ingredients, except for the salt and pepper, puff pastry and glaze.

▲ Season to taste and place in a buttered pie dish. Cover with puff pastry. Glaze with milk or a beaten egg, and place in a very hot oven for 15-20 minutes.

TOP Fishermen inspect their nets preparatory to a day's trawling; RIGHT, gathering seaweed – a common sight in 19th-century times and still a traditional delicacy.

Sea Bass Cooked with Seaweed in a Paper Case

COOKING TIME: 30 MINUTES

INGREDIENTS

1.5 kg/3 lb sea bass

Salt and pepper

15 ml/1 tbsp each of root fennel, shallots and chopped herbs

450 g/1 lb fresh seaweed (see Seaweed)

1 glass dry white wine

FOR THE SAUCE:

1 sweet red pepper

1 bulb of fennel

2 tomatoes (plum type, if available)

30 ml/2 tbsp chopped fresh herbs – parsley, chives, chervil, fennel and tarragon

Lemon juice

Olive oil

Salt and pepper to taste

OVEN TEMPERATURE: 200°C/400°F/GAS MARK 6

▲ Preheat the oven. Gut, clean and season the sea bass.

▲ Place the chopped fennel, shallots and herbs in the middle of the fish. Wrap the fish in fresh seaweed and put in a parcel of greaseproof (waxed) paper. Before you close the paper parcel, sprinkle the sea bass with the white wine.

▲ Place on a baking tray in the oven for about 30 minutes.

▲ While the fish is cooking, skin and chop the tomatoes. Roast the pepper under the grill, peel and chop it finely. Chop the fennel into small pieces and combine with the tomatoes, pepper and herbs in a bowl. Mix well and add some lemon juice, olive oil, salt and pepper.

▲ Serve the sea bass hot on a bed of seaweed with the sauce in a separate bowl.

Ray with Brown Butter Sauce

COOKING TIME: 20 MINUTES

INGREDIENTS

900 g/2 lb ray wings or any flat fish fillets
60-90 ml/4-6 tbsp unsalted butter
15 ml/1 tbsp chopped capers
60 ml/4 tbsp white wine vinegar
Black pepper and salt to taste

▲ Poach the ray wings in water which has a few drops of vinegar in it for about 10-15 minutes.

▲ Drain the fish and remove the skin – it comes off very easily at this stage. Keep warm in a low oven.

▲ Melt the butter in the pan over a medium heat until it turns brown – toss in the capers, then add the vinegar. Cook very fast for 30 seconds, then pour over the fish.

▲ Garnish with parsley and lemon wedges and serve with small new potatoes to soak up the delicious butter.

Plaice (Flounder) with Mustard Sauce

COOKING TIME: 20 MINUTES

INGREDIENTS

4 plaice or flounder fillets
2 shallots, chopped
30 ml/2 tbsp Dijon mustard
2/3 cup/150 ml/1/4 pt cream
Watercress

OVEN TEMPERATURE:
180°C/350°F/GAS MARK 4

▲ Preheat the oven. Butter a Pyrex or an enamel dish. Place the fish fillets in the dish.

▲ Mix the shallots, mustard and cream together. Pour over the plaice and bake in a moderate oven for 15-20 minutes.

▲ Serve with bunches of watercress.

Bantry Bay, in Cork, in another favourite fishing ground. Here, try your luck and spend an evening mackerel fishing from a quiet seaside harbour – marvellous sport and a wonderfully fresh, tasty catch.

Plaice (Flounder) with Mustard Sauce

This is a traditional way to serve fresh lobster. It is essential to make it with raw lobster. Get your fishmonger to kill the lobster, cut it lengthways, and remove all the meat, including the claw meat. This is difficult to do on your own at home. Make sure you keep the coral. This recipe serves 2.

Dublin Lawyer

COOKING TIME: 10 MINUTES

INGREDIENTS

1 fresh lobster, about 1.25 kg/2½ lb, cut into chunks, together with the coral

90 ml/6 tbsp butter

60 ml/4 tbsp Irish whiskey

⅔ cup/150 ml/¼ pt cream

Salt and pepper

▲ Heat the butter in a heavy pan until it froths, but do not brown it.

▲ Cook the lobster meat and the coral lightly for a few minutes.

▲ Warm the whiskey, set it alight, and flame the lobster.

▲ When the flames die down, add the cream. Heat for a few moments – on no account allow it to boil.

▲ Place the meat and sauce back into the lobster shells. Serve on a bed of chilled lettuce or on a bed of boiled rice.

Brown bread and lots of napkins are needed to enjoy these to the full – eat them with your fingers.

INGREDIENTS

675 g/1½ lb live large prawns (jumbo shrimp), with shells

½ cup/100 g/¼ lb garlic butter (made with unsalted butter)

Lemon wedges

Parsley sprigs

Dublin Bay Prawns in Garlic Butter

COOKING TIME: 10 MINUTES

▲ Boil some water and salt in a large pan. Plunge the prawns in the water. Bring back to the boil and cook for one minute.

▲ Drain the prawns and toss in hot garlic butter for 2-3 minutes. Serve decorated with lemon wedges and parsley.

Preparing Crab

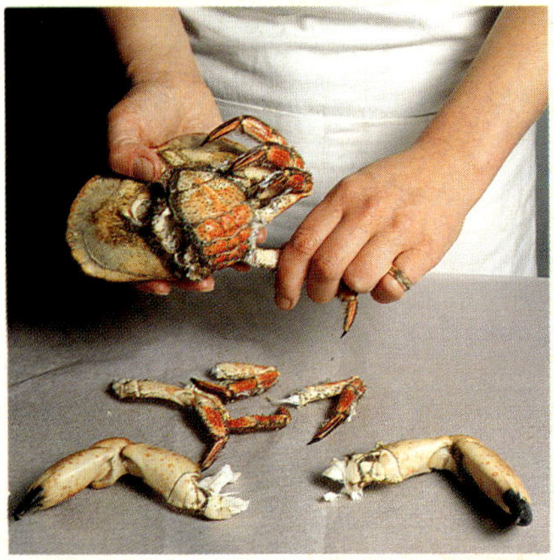

1 Turn the crab onto its back. Twist off the claws and then the legs – do not pull them.

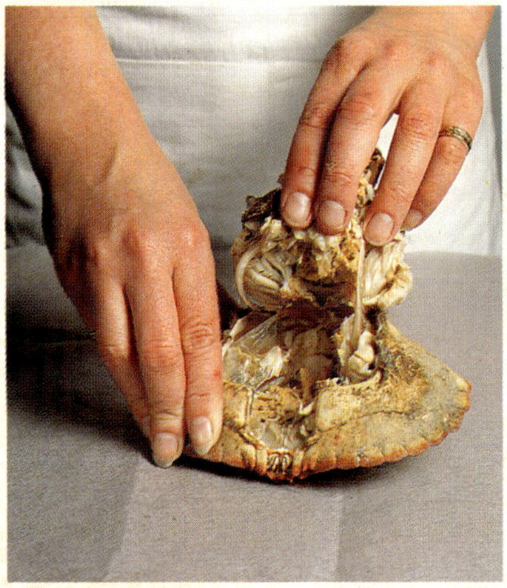

2 Pull the apron up from the pointed end near the mouth to remove the body from the shell.

3 Remove the dead men's fingers – these are soft and spongy and you will find them at the sides of the body. Remove the stomach sac – this lies behind the head.

4 Prise out any cartilaginous membrane from the shell and discard it.

5 Remove the brown meat from the shell and keep to one side.

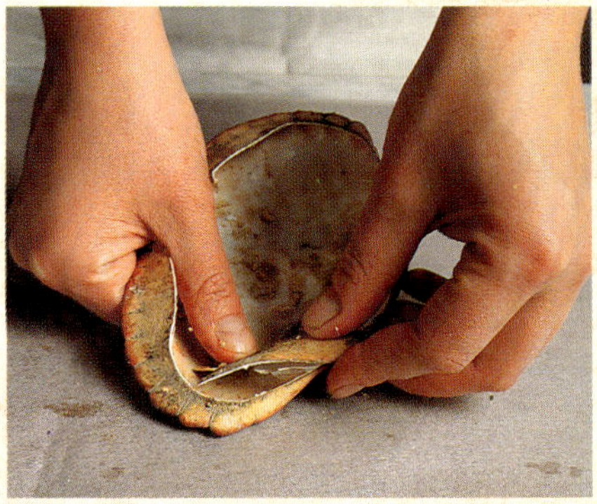

6 Using your thumbs, break the shell to enlarge and neaten the opening. Wash the shell thoroughly.

7 Remove the white meat from the body, claws and legs. Use a hammer or crackers to open the claws and legs. A skewer is also useful for extracting flesh from awkward corners.

Creamed Crab

Devilled Crab (for 4)

COOKING TIME: 15-20 MINUTES

INGREDIENTS

1 crab per person (cooked)
½ cup/100 g/¼ lb butter, melted
2 cups/100 g/¼ lb fresh breadcrumbs
20 ml/1 heaped tbsp Dijon mustard
Lemon juice
Pinch of cayenne pepper

OVEN TEMPERATURE:
180°C/350°F/GAS MARK 4

▲ Preheat the oven. Remove all the meat from the freshly cooked crabs (*see* Preparing Crab for method).
▲ Place the meat in a mixing bowl with the melted butter and fresh breadcrumbs. Add the mustard, lemon juice and cayenne. Mix very well.
▲ Stuff the mixture back into the crab shells and heat in a very hot oven for 15 minutes and finish under the grill (broiler) for a few minutes more. Serve very hot with lemon wedges.

Creamed Crab

PREPARATION TIME: 20 MINUTES

INGREDIENTS

225 g/½ lb freshly cooked crab meat
2 tomatoes, peeled and chopped
2 hard-boiled eggs, chopped
1¼ cups/300 ml/½ pt Green Mayonnaise (see Basic Recipes)
Juice of 1 lemon
Chopped chives and parsley
Salt and pepper

▲ Put all the ingredients in a bowl and mix well. Serve with chilled pieces of Cos (Romaine) lettuce, or in puff pastry cases.

Kedgeree

COOKING TIME: 30 MINUTES

INGREDIENTS

900 g/2 lb smoked haddock or cod
1 bay leaf
675 g/1½ lb basmati or long grain rice
225 g/½ lb unsalted butter
8 hard-boiled eggs
15 ml/1 tbsp good curry powder
1¼ cups/300 ml/½ pt béchamel sauce (see *Basic Recipes*)
Chopped coriander
Lemon slices

▲ Cover the fish with cold water and add a bay leaf. Bring to the boil and turn off the heat. Remove the fish and keep the water.

▲ Cook the rice in 100 g/¼ lb butter and the fish water, adding extra cold water, if necessary. There should be double the volume of water to rice. Cook the rice until most of the water has been absorbed and holes appear on the surface. Turn off the heat and cover – leave in a warm place or low oven until you deal with the fish.

▲ Remove all bones and skin from the fish. Shell and roughly chop the eggs. Melt the rest of the butter and add the curry powder. Cook for a couple of minutes and add the fish.

▲ Make the béchamel sauce (*see* Basic Recipes) and add to the fish and butter. Cook for 2 minutes. Then gently fold into the rice, which should now be perfectly cooked, making sure all the grains are equally coated. Then mix in the chopped hard-boiled eggs.

▲ Serve in a large warm bowl garnished with fresh coriander and lemon slices.

Kedgeree is an Anglo-Indian dish which is good for breakfast, lunch or supper. In Ireland, I remember it mainly as a breakfast dish – served on Sundays in country houses. It has happily outlasted the colonial connections.

Soused Herrings with Sour Cream

PREPARATION AND COOKING TIME:
20 MINUTES, + COOLING

INGREDIENTS

6 fresh herring fillets
1 large Spanish onion, sliced
6 bay leaves
18 whole black peppercorns
1¼ cups/300 ml/½ pt red wine vinegar mixed with water
1¼ cups/300 ml/½ pt sour cream
Fresh dill, chopped

OVEN TEMPERATURE:
170°C/325°F/GAS MARK 3

▲ Preheat the oven. Wash the herring fillets and pat them dry with kitchen paper.

▲ Place some of the thinly sliced onion, a bay leaf, and three whole peppercorns on each fish. Roll up the herrings with the tail-end away from you. Place in an ovenproof dish and cover with the vinegar and water mixture.

▲ Place in a moderate oven until the herrings are cooked – about 20 minutes. Let the fish cool in the liquid for several hours or overnight.

▲ Serve cold with a spoonful of sour cream garnished with chopped dill.

meat dishes

Roast Ribs of Beef with Béarnaise Sauce 58

Gaelic Steak 59

Wellington Beef 60

Beef in Guinness 61

Irish Spiced Beef 62

Salt Beef with Cabbage and Parsley Sauce 63

Beef Stew with Herb Dumplings 66

Rack of Lamb in a Mustard Crust with Mint Sauce or Jelly 67

Irish Stew 68

Mutton in Caper Sauce 69

Dublin Coddle 70

Braised Ham with Prunes 71

Roast Stuffed Pork Steak 72

Pork Ciste 73

LEFT *The luscious pastures of County Cork – ideal country for raising dairy and beef cattle, as well as sheep.*

INGREDIENTS

1.75 kg/4 lb beef rib
Sea salt and freshly ground black pepper
½ cup/100 g/¼ lb unsalted (sweet) butter

Roast Rib of Beef with Bearnaise Sauce

COOKING TIME: 40 MINUTES

▲ Season the rib of beef with salt and pepper and place in a heavy roasting pan. Melt the butter and cook in a hot oven, browning the meat on both sides. For rare meat, cook for 10 minutes per pound on each side. Remove the meat to a serving platter and keep warm.

▲ To make the sauce, in a small heavy saucepan melt 15 ml/1 tbsp of butter. Add the shallots. Cook slowly for about 10 minutes, then add the vinegar, half the tarragon and chervil, and salt and pepper to taste. Reduce the sauce to about 10 ml/2 tsp.

▲ Cool the mixture and add the egg yolks and the cold water. Mix with a whisk over a low heat or in a double boiler or saucepan. Make sure you amalgamate the eggs with the shallot mixture, but do not cook them or the sauce will be ruined.

▲ When the egg yolks look thick and creamy, gradually whisk the remaining butter in, making sure the sauce does not separate. If it gets too thick, add a little water.

▲ When the sauce is finished, add more chopped tarragon and chervil. Keep warm in the double boiler or double saucepan. (If the worst happens and the sauce separates, start again with a little water in a saucepan. Heat it continuously, adding small quantities of the sauce until it emulsifies again.)

▲ Carve the ribs and serve the sauce separately.

FOR THE BEARNAISE SAUCE:

1 cup/225 g/½ lb unsalted (sweet) butter, cut into cubes
4 shallots or green onions, finely chopped
45 ml/3 tbsp white wine vinegar
30 ml/2 tbsp fresh tarragon, chopped
2.5 ml/½ tsp chopped chervil
Pinch of ground black pepper and salt
4 egg yolks
30 ml/2 tbsp cold water

OVEN TEMPERATURE:
220°C/425°F/GAS MARK 7

Irish whiskey, with a kick all of its own, is a superb aperitif for pre-meal drinking.

Gaelic Steak

INGREDIENTS

225 g/½ lb sirloin steak per person
Garlic butter
Shot of Irish whiskey
Cream
Watercress
Salt and pepper

▲ Rub each side of the steak with the garlic butter. Place on a hot griddle, or in a heavy pan over a high heat. For rare steak, cook on each side for 3 minutes; allow 4 minutes each side for a medium steak and 5 minutes if you prefer your steak well-done.

▲ Then pour a shot of warmed whiskey over the steak and set alight. When the flames die down, put the steak on a hot plate.

▲ Add a little cream to the pan juices and cook over a fierce heat for a few minutes. Pour the sauce over the steak, season, and serve with sprigs of watercress.

I don't know if this dish was called after the Duke of Wellington or happened to be something he liked. It is rather an ersatz Irish dish as the Duke of Wellington was merely born in Ireland. However, it makes a very good hot or cold party dish.

Wellington Beef

PREPARATION AND COOKING TIME: 30 MINUTES

INGREDIENTS

450 g/1 lb flaky or puff pastry (see Basic Recipes)
1 whole piece of fillet steak (about 900 g/2 lb)
Salt and pepper
¾ cup/175 g/6 oz butter
450 g/1 lb mushrooms, finely chopped
1 medium onion, finely chopped
2 cloves of garlic, chopped
Mixed herbs
1 egg, beaten, to glaze

OVEN TEMPERATURE: 220°C/425°F/GAS MARK 7

▲ Preheat the oven. Make the flaky pastry (*see* Basic Recipes) and chill in the refrigerator.

▲ Trim the fillet and season with salt and pepper. Rub with butter and roast in a hot oven for about 10 minutes.

▲ Chop the mushrooms, onion, garlic and herbs and cook in the rest of the butter. Drain well and put in a layer on the top of the fillet.

▲ Roll out the pastry large enough to fit around the beef and meet at the top. Brush beaten egg on the edges of the pastry and squeeze together with your fingers. If you are worried about the pastry opening during cooking, put the seam under the beef and decorate the top with pastry leaves made from the trimmings. Brush all over with beaten egg and bake for about 20 minutes or until the pastry is golden. Serve hot or cold.

My goodness, my Guinness! This is Ireland's world-famous stout, hugely popular at home, where it still comes in traditional wooden casks, and abroad.

Beef in Guinness

COOKING TIME: ABOUT 2 HOURS

INGREDIENTS

900 g-1.5 kg/2-3 lb beef skirt
Seasoned flour
Oil or dripping
2 onions, sliced
4 cloves of garlic, whole
3 carrots, sliced
1 large bunch of fresh herbs
Salt and pepper
2½ cups/600 ml/1 pt beef stock (see *Basic Recipes*)
2 bottles of Guinness
1 oyster per person (optional)

▲ Cut the beef into large chunks and dip in seasoned flour. Fry in hot oil or dripping. Fry and brown the onions and garlic.

▲ Place the meat, onions and other vegetables in a casserole dish. Add the herbs and seasoning, and cover with beef stock. Bring to the boil, cover, and cook over a low heat for 1½ hours. Then add the Guinness, bring to the boil and simmer for another 30 minutes.

▲ Lift the meat out of the sauce with a slotted spoon and serve; reduce the sauce to half the quantity over a high heat. Pour it over the beef again, season to taste, and add the oysters, if liked.

▲ Serve with wedges of white crusty bread with mustard and a pint of Guinness.

Spiced beef is traditional Christmas fare in Ireland. As a child I remember it appearing in the butchers shops a few weeks before Christmas, looking like chocolate logs decorated with holly and red ribbons. It is, however, very simple to prepare.

INGREDIENTS

20 cloves
2 pieces of mace
10 ml/2 tsp allspice or cinnamon
6 shallots
10 ml/2 tsp saltpetre (preserving agent)
30 ml/2 tbsp brown sugar
450 g/1 lb coarse sea salt
5 ml/1 tsp black pepper
1 large joint of beef 3.25-3.5 kg/7-8 lb
2-3 bay leaves
Nutmeg, grated
2 bottles Guinness or brown beer

Irish Spiced Beef

PREPARATION AND COOKING TIME:
AT LEAST 8 DAYS + 5-6 HOURS

▲ Put all the spices in a coffee grinder and grind to a powder.
▲ Put the shallots, spices, saltpetre, sugar, salt and meat in a shallow earthenware or Pyrex dish. Rub the salt and spices into the meat, grate nutmeg over it, and leave for a week in a cool place.
▲ Turn the meat once a day and rub the spices into the meat again.
▲ After at least a week wrap the meat in muslin and simmer in hot water for about 5-6 hours with the bay leaves and nutmeg. About half an hour before the end of the cooking, add 2 bottles of Guinness or brown beer.
▲ When cooked, remove from the liquid and cool, pressed between two plates for several hours or overnight. Serve thinly sliced. It is always served cold, on Christmas Eve or St Stephen's Day (26 December)

Ireland's dairy and beef cattle need careful nurturing to maintain their quality. The hay here will be used as winter fodder.

Like smoked ham, salt beef needs to be soaked in cold water the night before cooking.

INGREDIENTS

2.75 kg/6 lb salted silverside roast, uncooked
1 Savoy or curly cabbage, shredded
1 onion, roughly chopped
2 bay leaves
Parsley Sauce (see Basic Recipes)

Salt Beef with Cabbage and Parsley Sauce

PREPARATION AND COOKING TIME: OVERNIGHT + 2 HOURS

▲ Discard the soaking water, put the beef into a large pan and cover with fresh cold water. Bring to the boil and throw the water away, then cover with more fresh cold water.
▲ Poach with the onion and bay leaves for about 2 hours. Ten minutes before the end of the cooking add the shredded Savoy or curly cabbage.
▲ Remove the beef, cut into slices and arrange on a hot platter. Surround with the drained cabbage and cover with parsley sauce.
▲ On a separate tray serve pickled cucumbers and mustard.

MAGIC CRYSTAL FROM WATERFORD

At the Waterford Crystal factory, the dream of reviving Ireland's 19th-century glass-making tradition has been fully realized, as the showroom examples here demonstrate. The sign (RIGHT) indicates the number of foreign visitors the factory attracts.

INGREDIENTS

900 g/2 lb lean stewing beef (either chuck, skirt or flank), cut into large chunks
Seasoned flour
Beef dripping, fat or oil
2 onions, peeled and chopped
2 carrots, peeled and chopped
2 cloves of garlic, peeled and chopped
1 turnip, peeled and chopped
2 sticks of celery, chopped
2 tomatoes, peeled, seeded and chopped
3 floury potatoes, peeled and chopped
1 large bunch of fresh herbs
Salt, pepper, whole allspice
2½ cups/600 ml/1 pt beef stock (see Basic Recipes)

Beef Stew with Herb Dumplings

COOKING TIME: 2 HOURS 30 MINUTES

▲ Dip the meat into seasoned flour and seal in hot beef dripping or oil. Then fry the onions and the rest of the vegetables.

▲ Place the meat on a bed of vegetables in a large saucepan, or casserole. Stuff the bunch of herbs in the middle, season and cover with well-flavoured beef stock. Cover and cook over a low heat for 2 hours.

▲ While the stew is cooking make the dumplings, first by mixing all the dry ingredients together, then by adding the beaten egg to bind.

▲ Divide the mixture into small pieces, about the size of a walnut. Roll between floured palms into an even shape.

▲ Cook in boiling stock or salted water for 15-20 minutes, then add to the stew 15-20 minutes before it is fully cooked.

▲ Serve on a hot plate garnished with parsley.

TO MAKE THE DUMPLINGS:

COOKING TIME: 20 MINUTES

90 ml/6 tbsp self-raising (rising) flour
1 cup/2 oz fresh breadcrumbs
50 g/2 oz suet (preferably vegetarian)
15 ml/1 tbsp or to taste, chopped mixed herbs
Salt and pepper
Finely chopped shallots (optional)
1 egg, beaten
Stock or water

INGREDIENTS

2 well-trimmed racks of lamb (best end of neck) – allow 3 chops per portion

½ cup/100 g/¼ lb butter

225/½ lb breadcrumbs

30 ml/2 tbsp Dijon mustard

5 ml/1 tsp rosemary

1 onion, finely chopped

Mint sauce, or 15 ml/1 tbsp mint or redcurrant jelly per person

OVEN TEMPERATURE:
220°C/425°F/GAS MARK 7

Rack of Lamb in a Mustard Crust with Mint Sauce or Jelly

PREPARATION AND COOKING TIME:
25 MINUTES

▲ Preheat the oven. Make sure any surplus fat is trimmed from the meat.

▲ Make the crust by melting the butter and mixing all the other ingredients into it. Allow the mixture to chill in the refrigerator for about 15 minutes. Cut the racks of lamb into portions of three cutlets. Coat the back of the chops with a layer of the sauce about ½ in/1 cm thick.

▲ Place the racks in a roasting pan in a hot oven for about 10 minutes.

▲ Serve with mint sauce, mint jelly or redcurrant jelly.

This recipe is a classic Irish stew. Paul Bocuse describes it as one of the world's great classic dishes. It is a white stew and should not even have carrots in it, although carrots or braised red cabbage are the traditional accompaniments.

Irish Stew

COOKING TIME: 3 HOURS

▲ Preheat the oven, if using. In a large heavy pan place one-third of the sliced onions and the sliced potatoes. On this layer place half of the meat, season, and add half of the remaining onions and the sliced potatoes. Season and add the garlic, bouquet garni, and the rest of the meat. Finish with a layer of the sliced onions and potatoes, and season with more salt and pepper. Just cover the meat and vegetables with water, bring to the boil and cover with greaseproof (waxed) paper and a lid. Cook slowly on top of the stove or in a low oven for an hour.

▲ Peel the new potatoes and the small onions.

▲ Take the stew from the oven or off the heat after an hour – the onions and the potatoes should be almost falling apart. Mash them a little bit and add the new potatoes and whole onions to the stew.

▲ The meat may be removed now and put back in again before the end of cooking to prevent it falling off the bone. This is for aesthetic purposes only, as it does not affect the flavour. At this point if the stew is too thick add some water. Cover again and cook for another hour. Serve in hot bowls garnished with parsley.

INGREDIENTS

1.5 kg/3 lb best end of neck of lamb
900 g/2 lb floury potatoes, peeled and sliced
900 g/2 lb onions, peeled and sliced
Salt and pepper
3 cloves of garlic
1 large bouquet garni, including celery tops
12 small new potatoes
12 small onions
Chopped parsley

OVEN TEMPERATURE, IF USED: 150°C/300°F/GAS MARK 2

Irish lamb perfectly complements the other ingredients in classic stews and casseroles.

One of the reasons why this excellent dish is rarely seen today is probably due to the scarcity of mutton. Mutton is now considered the poor relation of lamb. I don't see the reason for this, as I consider it has a much better flavour, and is as good hot or cold. A side product of poaching the mutton in the following recipe is a wonderful mutton broth (or see Mutton Broth with Barley).

Mutton in Caper Sauce

COOKING TIME: 2 HOURS 20 MINUTES

▲ Make sure there is no surplus fat on the meat. Put into a deep, heavy saucepan and cover with cold water. Bring slowly to the boil and simmer for about 15 minutes. Skim off any scum that appears on the surface.

▲ Add the scrubbed and peeled vegetables, herbs and seasoning. Cover and simmer gently for about 2 hours.

▲ Make the sauce by melting the butter and adding the flour to make a roux. Cook for 1 minute. Add 2½ cups/600 ml/1 pt of strained stock from the meat pan, gradually stirring to avoid lumps. Boil for 3 minutes and add the capers. Season with salt and pepper. (Be careful with the salt as the capers may be salty enough – I once nearly poisoned people by adding extra salt when the capers had been preserved in brine.)

▲ Finally, add some cream and heat, but do not boil again.

▲ Serve the mutton cut into thick slices on a platter. Surround with the cooked vegetables and cover with the caper sauce.

INGREDIENTS

1 boned and rolled leg of mutton (about 1.75kg/4 lb in weight)
900 g/2 lb whole tiny carrots, scrubbed
900 g/2 lb pickling, or medium-sized, onions
450 g/1 lb small turnips
2 cloves of garlic
Bunch of thyme, rosemary and bay leaf
Salt and pepper
Water to cover

FOR THE SAUCE:

30 ml/2 tbsp butter
30 ml/2 tbsp flour
2½ cups/1 pt mutton stock (see below)
Small jar capers
Cream
Salt and pepper

Coddle was traditionally served when 'the Men' came in from the pub on a Saturday night.

INGREDIENTS

900 g/2 lb pure pork sausages
Seasoned flour
A little bacon fat or sunflower oil
450 g/1 lb rashers of bacon or knuckle of ham
2 large onions, sliced
2 cloves of garlic
2 carrots, thickly sliced
4 large potatoes, thickly sliced
Bunch of fresh herbs
Black pepper
Cider
Chopped parsley

Dublin Coddle

COOKING TIME: ABOUT 1 HOUR

▲ Dip the sausages into seasoned flour and seal in hot bacon fat or oil. Soften the onions and whole garlic cloves in the oil.

▲ Place the sausages, bacon and onions in a large saucepan with thickly sliced potatoes and carrots. Bury a large bunch of fresh herbs in the middle and cover with cider.

▲ Cook over a moderate heat for at least an hour, but do not boil.

▲ Garnish with parsley. Serves 6 in deep dishes, together with soda bread. Wash down with mugs of Guinness.

The night before using the ham, soak it in cold water to remove the surplus salt. Saw off the knuckle and use for stock.
The prunes must also be soaked the night before.

INGREDIENTS

2.75 kg/6 lb smoked (Limerick) ham, lightly cured
450 g/1 lb large whole prunes
1 apple, stuck with cloves
2½ cups/600 ml/1 pt cider
Juniper berries

OVEN TEMPERATURE:
180°C/350°F/GAS MARK 4

Braised Ham with Prunes

PREPARATION AND COOKING TIME:
OVERNIGHT + 2 HOURS

▲ Preheat the oven. Remove the ham from the cold water and place in a large pan with fresh cold water. Bring slowly to the boil and throw the water away.

▲ Place in a casserole, or deep baking dish, surrounded by the drained prunes, apple and juniper berries. Pour the cider over the ham and loosely cover with foil. Cook in a moderate oven, basting every 15 minutes. Allow 20 minutes to the pound (about 2 hours).

▲ Remove the skin when the ham is cooked and serve on a plate with a few prunes and some parsley or onion sauce (*see* Soft-Boiled Eggs in Ramekins with Onion Sauce).

Pork steak is a cut of meat once unique to Ireland, but it may now be found in other butchers under the name pork fillet. It is lean and moist and is at its best stuffed and roasted.
I like to use about 900 g/2 lb of fillet or pork steak left whole.

Roast Stuffed Pork Steak

COOKING TIME: 1 HOUR 15 MINUTES

INGREDIENTS

900 g/2 lb pork steak or fillet
Salt
30 ml/2 tbsp butter
30 ml/2 tbsp water or cider

FOR THE STUFFING:

900 g/2 lb cooked mashed potato
60 ml/4 tbsp butter
1 onion, finely chopped
2 large cooking (tart) apples
1 handful of sage and thyme, chopped
Salt and pepper

OVEN TEMPERATURE:
180°C/350°F/GAS MARK 4

▲ Make the stuffing first. Mash the potatoes. Add the butter, chopped onion, chopped apple, herbs, salt and pepper. Mix well and check the seasoning.

▲ Place the meat in a ring shape in a casserole or roasting pan. Put the stuffing in the middle. Rub the meat with salt and butter and put a little water or cider in the pan. Cover loosely with foil and place in a moderate oven for about 1 hour.

▲ This dish is marvellous hot or cold and may be served with roasted apples. Serve cut into little steaks or medallions with the stuffing and a roasted apple. The pan juices may be reduced and poured over the steaks. It makes a good alternative to turkey for Christmas dinner and goes very well with all the traditional Christmas vegetables.

The smart check frontage of this Kilkenny victuallers complements the fresh meat to be found in its cool interior.

Pork Ciste

COOKING TIME: 2 HOURS

INGREDIENTS

6 lean pork chops
2 pork kidneys
1 large onion
2 carrots
60 ml/4 tbsp butter
1/3 cup/50 g/2 oz raisins and sultanas (golden raisins)
15 ml/1 tbsp parsley, chopped
15 ml/1 tbsp sage and thyme, chopped
Salt and pepper
Approx 2½ cups/600 ml/1 pt pork stock, or cider

SUET CRUST

1½ cups/225 g/½ lb self-raising (rising) flour
Pinch of salt
100 g/¼ lb grated suet or vegetarian suet (lighter)
2/3 cup/150 ml/¼ pt milk
Pinch of cardamom seeds, crushed
15 ml/1 tbsp cooking apple, grated
5 ml/1 tsp mixed spice

▲ Trim any fat off the pork chops. Peel and cut any tubes off the kidneys and slice them. Peel and slice the vegetables.

▲ Fry the meat in the butter over a high heat, but without burning the butter. Remove to a casserole dish and fry the vegetables.

▲ Arrange the chops around the edge of the casserole dish, arranging the kidneys and the vegetables in the middle with the dried fruit and herbs. Add enough stock or cider to cover the vegetables. Cover with a lid, bring to the boil and simmer for 30 minutes.

▲ Make the suet pastry. Mix all the dry ingredients in a bowl and add the milk. Knead into a fairly stiff dough, then roll it out to fit into the casserole dish and press it down over the meat and vegetables. Cover with greaseproof (waxed) paper and a lid. Simmer for 1½ hours.

▲ To serve, loosen around the pastry lid and cut into six portions. Place one chop and some kidney and vegetable mixture on each plate with the crust, or *ciste,* on top. *Ciste* (pronounced kishte) merely means 'cake' in Irish.

Poultry and Game

Poached Turkey with Celery Sauce 76

Michaelmas Goose with Red Cabbage, Apple and Chestnuts 77

Chicken and Mushroom Pie 78

Wild Duck with Spiced Oranges 79

Game Pie 80

Pigeon and Bacon Pie with Stuffed Apples 81

Braised Pheasant with Apple and Cream Sauce 82

Hare Pudding 83

LEFT *Ducks, with other poultry, are all part and parcel of the typical Irish farm scene.*

Turkey tends to be very dry, a problem this recipe overcomes. It makes a very welcome change from the ubiquitous roast stuffed turkey.

INGREDIENTS

Giblet stock
4.5-5.5 kg/10-12 lb turkey
450 g/1 lb streaky bacon, cubed
4 carrots, sliced
4 small onions, stuck with cloves
Celery, chopped
Bunch of herbs
Assorted vegetables
Watercress

Poached Turkey with Celery Sauce

COOKING TIME: 4 HOURS + 15 MINUTES

▲ Make a stock from the giblets, or use some white stock (*see* Basic Recipes). Wipe the turkey inside and out. In a very large pan, heat the bacon and vegetables.

▲ Place the turkey on top of the vegetables, cover with the stock and drop in the herbs. Cook the bird very slowly for 4 hours. Turn it a couple of times during the cooking. When it is ready, keep in a warm oven.

▲ For the sauce, make a roux with the flour and butter. Slowly add the strained turkey stock and stir while bringing this to the boil. Boil for about 3 minutes, then add the celery and parsley. Finish with a little cream, but do not boil.

▲ Take the turkey from the oven and remove the skin. Cut the turkey into pieces and serve on a platter with other cooked vegetables, including Brussels sprouts, pickling onions, carrots or other preferred vegetables.

▲ Pour the celery sauce over the turkey and garnish with watercress.

FOR THE SAUCE:

30 ml/2 tbsp butter
30 ml/2 tbsp flour
2½ cups/600 ml/1 pt turkey stock (see Basic Recipes)
1 large head boiled celery, chopped
15 ml/1 tbsp parsley, chopped
Cream

OVEN TEMPERATURE:
180°C/350°F/GAS MARK 4

Michaelmas Goose with Red Cabbage, Apple and Chestnuts

COOKING TIME: ABOUT 2½ HOURS

INGREDIENTS

1 young goose 3.5-4 kg/8-10 lb
Salt
15 ml/1 tbsp goose or duck fat
30 ml/2 tbsp water
Seasoned flour

FOR STUFFING:

900 g/2 lb potatoes
2 onions, chopped
Goose liver, chopped
30 ml/2 tbsp butter
1 bunch of spring (green) onions
5 ml/1 tsp each chopped thyme and sage
Salt and pepper

FOR RED CABBAGE:

1 red cabbage
1 Spanish onion
60 ml/4 tbsp unsalted (sweet) butter
225 g/½ lb cooked chestnuts
2 cooking (tart) apples
Salt, pepper, 5 juniper berries
Water or cider

FOR APPLE SAUCE:

3 cooking or tart apples
30 ml/2 tbsp water
15 ml/1 tbsp brown sugar
15 ml/1 tbsp butter
Grated orange peel

OVEN TEMPERATURE:
180°C/350°F/GAS MARK 4

▲ First make the stuffing. Scrub the potatoes and boil in salted water in their skins. Peel and mash them while they are still hot.

▲ Soften the onions and liver in the butter. Add to the mashed potatoes, then sprinkle over the spring (green) onions, herbs and seasoning. Add a lot of freshly ground black pepper.

▲ Clean out the goose and wipe with kitchen paper. Put the stuffing in the belly of the bird and sew up the vent with thick sewing thread. (If you are cooking a goose at Christmas, it is a different beast and very fat – cook the stuffing separately in a baking dish.) Rub the salt and fat over the goose and place in a roasting tin with the water.

▲ Bake in a moderate oven for 2 hours. Baste from time to time. In the last half hour, dredge with flour and allow to become crisp. (If you are cooking a goose at Christmas, you do not need to baste it – as it has a lot of fat. Cook it on a wire rack above a roasting pan to catch the fat dripping from the bird.)

▲ To make the traditional red cabbage, slice the onion and shred the cabbage. Cook in the butter in a large pot until soft. Add the cooked and peeled chestnuts together with the apples. Put the pot in the oven with the goose. Add the seasoning and a little water or cider and serve with the goose and apple sauce.

▲ Apple sauce is always served with goose in Ireland. Peel and core the apples. Heat the water and sugar together in a saucepan, and add the apples. Boil until they disintegrate. Mash, add the butter and grated orange peel, mix well and return to the boiling point.

Since medieval times, geese have been a traditional Irish favourite, though today they are a rich man's, rather than a poor man's, luxury.

INGREDIENTS

1 good-sized boiling chicken
1 Spanish onion
Bouquet garni
Carrots, celery and leeks
Dry white wine (optional)
450 g/1 lb button mushrooms, or, if available, wild mushrooms
Knob of butter, softened and worked with 15 ml/1 tbsp flour
15 ml/1 tbsp fresh herbs, including tarragon
450 g/1 lb flaky pastry (see Basic Recipes)
1 egg, beaten

OVEN TEMPERATURE: 220°C/425°F/GAS MARK 7

Chicken and Mushroom Pie

COOKING TIME: 1 HOUR 30 MINUTES

▲ Place the chicken in a pot with the onion, bouquet garni and vegetables. Cover with water and some dry white wine, if you have any.

▲ When the chicken is cooked, remove it from the pot and reserve the stock. Take off all the skin and remove the bones and any tough sinews. Cut the chicken into bite-sized pieces.

▲ Sauté the mushrooms in a little butter. Remove from the butter and place in a pie dish, together with the prepared chicken.

▲ Into the pan juices from the mushrooms, gradually add 2½ cups/ 600 ml/1 pt or more of the reserved chicken stock. Cook for a few minutes over a high heat. Thicken with a knob of butter worked together with 1 tbsp of flour. Add the fresh herbs and seasoning and pour over the chicken and mushrooms.

▲ Roll out the flaky pastry. Cover the contents to the edges of the baking dish, and brush an egg glaze on the pie. Cook in a hot oven until golden brown.

In common with other game birds, wild duck must be hung for about three days, until the skin has a greenish tinge to it.

As well as oranges, tiny clementines are delicious treated this way. Keep the spiced fruit for about 2 months before using.

Wild Duck with Spiced Oranges

COOKING TIME: 40-45 MINUTES

INGREDIENTS

2 wild duck
60 ml/4 tbsp butter
1¼ cups/300 ml/½ pt warmed port
Juice of 1 orange
Salt and freshly ground pepper
Bunch of watercress

OVEN TEMPERATURE:
200°C/400°F/GAS MARK 6

FOR THE SPICED ORANGES:

10 large thin-skinned oranges
2½ cups/600 ml/1 pt white wine vinegar
1.25 kg/2½ lb cane or loaf sugar
2 cinnamon sticks
1.75 ml/¼ tsp powdered cloves
6 blades of mace

▲ Preheat the oven. Rub the birds with butter and roast in a hot oven for 30 minutes, 20 minutes to cook 'pink'. Add the warmed port and put back in the oven for 10 minutes. Remove the birds from the pan to a serving platter and keep warm. Add the orange juice to the pan and cook over a fierce heat until the liquid is reduced.

▲ Pour the juices over the birds and decorate with sprigs of watercress. Serve with spiced oranges.

▲ To make the oranges, slice them about ¼-in/5-mm thick. Lay them in a pan or skillet and just cover with water.

▲ Simmer until the orange peel is tender, then take off the heat. In a saucepan, put the vinegar, sugar and spices and boil together for about 10 minutes.

▲ Drain the oranges and keep the liquor. Lay half the oranges in the syrup, making sure it covers the slices. Simmer for 30-40 minutes, until the fruit turns clear. Lift out into a dish, and put the remaining oranges into the pan. If the syrup does not cover them, add some of the orange liquor. Cook as before.

▲ Turn everything into a glass bowl and leave overnight. If the syrup is thin, remove the oranges with a slotted spoon and boil the liquid in a saucepan until reduced and thick. If the syrup is thick, just bring the fruit and liquid to the boil again and put into clean jars. Tie covers on when cool. If you do not have enough syrup to cover the oranges, boil up some more in the same proportions as before and fill the jars with it.

Serves 8-10. It is not really worth making a game pie for less than eight people.

Game Pie

COOKING TIME: 2 HOURS

INGREDIENTS

900g-1.25 kg/2-2½ lb stewing venison, or a mixture of rabbit and venison
225-350 g/8-12 oz pheasant, partridge or pigeon
1 onion
2 leeks
1 turnip
2 carrots
Bouquet garni
100 g/¼ lb butter
100 g/¼ lb shallots, chopped
225 g/½ lb mushrooms, chopped (100 g/¼ lb, if dried)
225 g/½ lb streaky bacon rashers
225 g/½ lb veal, ham or pork
100 g/¼ lb chicken livers
30 ml/2 tbsp chopped thyme
Savory, tarragon and parsley
Zest of 1 orange
Salt and freshly ground pepper
Pinch of powdered cloves
Pinch of nutmeg
2 cups/100 g/4 oz fresh breadcrumbs
1 egg, beaten
1 glass Madeira or port
5 hard-boiled eggs, chopped
450-675 g/1-1½ lb shortcrust or hot water pastry (see Basic Recipes)
Beaten egg to glaze

OVEN TEMPERATURE: 190°C/375°F/GAS MARK 5

▲ First of all make the stock. Put any bones you have, from whichever bird you use, together with the venison trimmings in a pot. Add the onions, leeks, carrots and turnip, with enough water to cover. Submerge the bouquet garni and simmer while you prepare the rest of the pie.

▲ In 60 ml/4 tbsp of the butter, fry the jointed birds until cooked 'pink'. Remove. In a little more butter fry the shallots and mushrooms.

▲ Preheat the oven. Line a 10-12-in/25-30-cm pie dish with half the rashers of bacon. Mince the rest of the bacon with the veal, ham or pork. Add 100 g/¼ lb of chicken livers and the reserved livers from the birds used in the pie. Put the minced meat into a basin and mix with the fried shallots and mushrooms, herbs, orange rind, salt, pepper and spices. Add the breadcrumbs, the whole egg and the Madeira. Mix well. If the mixture is too dry add some stock.

▲ Now begin filling the pie dish. Put a layer of the game joints over the rashers. Season and sprinkle with parsley. Add a layer of hard-boiled eggs, and then some of the forcemeat, rolled into balls. Continue the layers until full, cover with foil and bake for up to an hour.

▲ Take out of the oven and cool. If it has gone a bit dry add some stock. Put a pie funnel in the middle of the filling, cover with shortcrust pastry and let some of the funnel protrude. Glaze with egg and cook in a hot oven until the pastry is golden brown. Serve hot, or cold.

ABOVE RIGHT *Irish ingenuity knows no bounds when it comes to food, as this mobile cafeteria, complete with Egon Ronay recommendation, shows.*

Pigeon and Bacon Pie with Stuffed Apples

COOKING TIME: 80 MINUTES

INGREDIENTS

4 pigeons
60 ml/4 tbsp butter
2½ cups/600 ml/1 pt stock (see Basic Recipes)
1 large onion, chopped
225 g/½ lb sliced mushrooms
225 g/½ lb bacon
Pepper
4 hard-boiled eggs, chopped
15 ml/1 tbsp parsley, chopped
Marsala or red wine
Shortcrust or flaky pastry, to cover (see Basic Recipes)
Beaten egg

OVEN TEMPERATURE:
220°C/425°F/GAS MARK 7,
THEN 170°C/325°F/GAS MARK 3

▲ Preheat the oven. Cut the pigeons in half and brown in the butter. Simmer for just over an hour in the stock.

▲ Sauté the onions, mushrooms and chopped bacon in some butter. Place in a pie dish with the drained pigeons. Season with pepper and add the chopped hard-boiled eggs and parsley and enough stock mixed with Marsala or red wine to cover.

▲ Put a rim of the pastry of your choice around the edge of the dish. Brush it with beaten egg and cover with a lid of pastry.

▲ Put into a hot oven for 10 minutes to cook the pastry. Then reduce the heat and cook for 1 hour. If the pastry looks like it is overcooking, cover it with paper. Serve with stuffed apples or fresh pears, if preferred.

Stuffed Apples

INGREDIENTS

6 medium-sized Cox's or other sharp eating apples
Unsalted (sweet) butter
Brown sugar, powdered cloves and mixed spice, combined to taste

▲ Core the apples and stuff with a mixture of unsalted butter, brown sugar and spices. Cook with the pigeon pie when the pastry lid goes on.

Braised Pheasant with Apple and Cream Sauce

COOKING TIME: 45-50 MINUTES

INGREDIENTS

1 brace of pheasant
60 ml/4 tbsp butter
Chopped thyme, sage and rosemary
2 cooking apples
2 eating apples
1¼ cups/300 ml/½ pt cider
1¼ cups/300 ml/½ pt cream or crème fraîche
Salt and pepper
Parsley and chives to garnish

▲ Brown the pheasants in some of the butter. Remove the pheasants. Cut them in half and rub with the chopped herbs.

▲ Peel and slice the apples, and fry in the rest of the butter. Put the pheasants and the apples in a casserole, and pour over the cider. Cover the casserole and cook for about 40 minutes on the top of the oven.

▲ Remove the pheasants from the liquid and reduce the sauce. Then add the cream and heat just to boiling point, but do not boil unless you are using crème fraîche.

▲ Pour over the pheasants and garnish with parsley and chives.

ABOVE RIGHT

The Irish love of hunting and other field sports is world renowned and hare coursing is one of the many such activities that take place in suitable countryside.

Hare Pudding

COOKING TIME: OVER 4 HOURS

INGREDIENTS

6 rashers bacon
1 young hare, cut into pieces
Seasoned flour
1 onion, chopped
2 cloves of garlic, crushed
Mixed chopped fresh herbs
Salt and freshly ground black pepper
1¼ cups/300 ml/½ pt beef or game stock (see Basic Recipes)
1 glass port
Redcurrant jelly

TO MAKE THE SUET PASTRY:

1½ cups/225 g/½ lb self-raising (rising) flour
Pinch of salt
100 g/¼ lb shredded suet or vegetarian suet
Cold water

▲ Make the pastry first. Sift the flour and salt together. Add the suet and rub in with the fingers for a couple of minutes. Add cold water until you get a light dough. Knead lightly on a floured board. Make into a small ball. Roll out and use at once – it does not need to 'rest' in the refrigerator.

▲ Roll the pastry out to ¾ in/2 cm thickness and line a pudding basin with it. Cut the rinds off the bacon and line the bottom and sides of the basin. Dip the pieces of hare in seasoned flour and seal in hot fat. Soften the onions and place in the pudding basin with the pieces of hare. Add the garlic, herbs and seasoning and cover with the stock and port. Roll out the rest of the suet pastry and cover the pudding. Trim the edges and press down well at the join. Cover with greaseproof (waxed) paper and tie around with string.

▲ Steam or boil for 4 hours. Serve in the basin with a white napkin tied around it. Pass the redcurrant jelly in a jug.

Vegetables and Salads

Seaweed – Carrageen, Dulse and Sloke 86

Seaweed Salad 87

Sorrel-Stuffed Turnips 88

Colcannon 88

Boxty on the Griddle 89

Stuffed Onions 90

Salsify Fritters 90

Potato and Celeriac Purée 91

Champ or Cally 91

Sweet and Sour Red Cabbage 93

Potato Cakes 93

Mixed Vegetable Salad with Irish Dressing 94

Michaelmas Salad 95

LEFT *Rich fields, full of produce – a typically Irish scene. Down to the smallest cottage, all Irish country dwellers have their kitchen gardens, while, on farms, vegetable crops are frequently raised on a commercial scale.*

Seaweed and sea vegetables have been a staple in the Irish diet since prehistoric times. There are written details of dishes using seaweed as far back as the monastic period of the 5th and 6th centuries.
Carrageen, dulse and sloke are the most common seaweeds used in Ireland today.
Carrageen: *Carrageen is also known as 'sea moss' or 'Irish moss'. It is found on the rocks around the coast of Ireland. It is either purple or green, and it grows in short branches. Carrageen is used to thicken soups and mousses, and is a great alternative to gelatine for vegetarians.*
Dulse: *Also known as 'dillisk', it has a reddish-brown tint and is found on all the coasts of Ireland. It is often eaten dried, chewed like tobacco, or added to soups and stews. It needs to be cooked for a long time.*
Sloke: *Cooked sloke is just like spinach – hence its alternative name, sea spinach. It, too, is found on rocks all around Ireland's craggy coasts, one of the chief features of which is the awe-inspiring Giant's Causeway in County Antrim (*RIGHT*)*

Sloke

▲ Wash well to remove all sand and grit. Soak for a few hours or overnight. Put in a pan with a little water and some butter. Cook very slowly for at least 4 hours, or over a pilot light for even longer. Serve with some lemon juice and young roast lamb.

Dulse

▲ Add dulse to fish or vegetable stews. Cook as follows. Wash the dulse to remove any bits of sand or grit. Cook in stock, or water, for 2 or 3 hours.
▲ If you want to serve it as a vegetable, strain it after cooking, put it back in the pan and cover with melted butter and black pepper.

Carrageen

COOKING TIME: 30 MINUTES + SETTING TIME

INGREDIENTS

7¼-15 ml/½-1 tbsp carrageen
2½ cups/600 ml/1 pt milk
Zest of 1 lemon
Salt
15 ml/1 tbsp sugar

▲ Cover the dried carrageen with cold water, and soak for 15 minutes. Place in a saucepan with the milk, lemon zest and salt. Bring to the boil and simmer until it coats the back of a spoon.
▲ Add the sugar and stir until dissolved. Strain into a wet mould and leave in the refrigerator to set. Turn onto a pretty dish, pipe with cream and serve with fruit.

Seaweed Salad

PREPARATION AND COOKING TIME:
ABOUT 20 MINUTES

INGREDIENTS

A handful of egg noodles
Small piece of root ginger
3 cloves of garlic
1 bunch of spring onions
1 leek
1 cos lettuce
Watercress
Handful of soaked seaweed
Soy sauce and oyster sauce
Toasted sesame seeds

▲ Cook the egg noodles and keep to one side.
▲ Shred all the vegetables and the seaweed, then stir-fry in a little oil for about 3 minutes. Add 15 ml/1 tbsp each of soy sauce and oyster sauce.
▲ Cook for another 2 minutes and then mix with the noodles.
▲ Arrange on a pretty white dish and scatter the sesame seeds on top. It is good warm or cold.

Colcannon is always served on Halloween. I remember eating huge platefuls of it for lunch. On Halloween, a silver coin was wrapped in paper and dropped into the colcannon. We would eat copious amounts of it for lunch until the money was found. After that we rapidly lost interest! Nevertheless it is a very satisfying winter dish. It is traditionally made with kale, but you may substitute green Savoy or curly cabbage.

Sorrel-Stuffed Turnips

COOKING TIME: 30 MINUTES

INGREDIENTS

6 medium-sized turnips

675-900 g/$1\frac{1}{2}$-2 lb sorrel

60 ml/4 tbsp butter

$1\frac{1}{4}$ cups/300 ml/$\frac{1}{2}$ pt béchamel sauce (see Basic Recipes)

Parsley

▲ Scrub the turnips and cook in boiling water until tender. Keep warm.

▲ Melt the butter in a pan and drop in the sorrel. It almost melts in the butter. Scoop out the middles of the turnips and chop into the sorrel.

▲ Pack the stuffing in the cavities of the turnips. Keep warm in the oven, mix a little parsley with the béchamel sauce, and pour some over each stuffed turnip.

Colcannon

COOKING TIME: ABOUT 20-25 MINUTES

INGREDIENTS

1.5 kg/3 lb potatoes

$\frac{3}{4}$ cup/175 g/6 oz butter

Milk

1 bunch of spring (green) onions or chives, finely chopped

450 g/1 lb kale or green cabbage, cooked and finely chopped

Salt and pepper

Grated nutmeg

▲ Cook and mash the potatoes. Add the butter and milk and beat until well creamed.

▲ Then add the finely chopped onions or chives and cooked kale or cabbage. Season well with the salt and pepper and nutmeg.

Boxty on the Griddle

INGREDIENTS

450 g/1 lb potatoes
1 parsnip
1 onion
5 ml/1 tsp baking powder
Salt and pepper
2 large eggs, beaten
A little mashed potato

▲ Peel and grate the potatoes and parsnip. Squeeze as much water as possible out of the potatoes. Finely chop the onion and add to the parsnip and potatoes. Then add all the other ingredients and mix well.

▲ Spoon the boxty onto a hot griddle and cook on both sides. Serve with bacon and eggs for breakfast or with apple sauce for high tea. Traditional boxty does not have parsnip in the recipe, but it gives a very good flavour to the pancake.

Salsify Fritters

Stuffed Onions

COOKING TIME: 2 HOURS

INGREDIENTS	FOR THE STUFFING:
6 large Spanish onions	*350 g/¾ lb chopped ham*
Butter	*2 cups/100 g/¼ lb fresh white breadcrumbs*
Breadcrumbs and grated cheese	*100 g/¼ lb fat streaky bacon*
Stock	*5 ml/1 tsp mixed sweet herbs*
	1 tomato, chopped and skinned
	Béchamel sauce (see Basic Recipes)

OVEN TEMPERATURE: 190°-200°C/375°-400°F/ GAS MARK 5 OR 6

▲ Preheat the oven. Cut the roots from the onions and remove the outer thin layer of skin. Cook the onions in a large pot of boiling salted water on top of the stove for about an hour. Remove from the water with a slotted spoon. Test with a skewer: they should be cooked, but not falling apart.
▲ With a sharp pointed knife cut a circle from the stem end of the onion. Then carefully remove the core of the onion. Do not remove so much that it collapses. Chop the core of the onions and mix with the stuffing ingredients and a little béchamel. Pack into the onions and mound the stuffing above the top of the onion into a dome shape.
▲ Place the onions in a baking dish with the butter. Sprinkle the tops with breadcrumbs and a little grated cheese. Bake for about 1 hour. If they appear to dry during the cooking, baste them with a little stock. Serve very hot.

Salsify Fritters

COOKING TIME: 15 MINUTES

INGREDIENTS

900 g/2 lb salsify
Juice of ½ lemon or 15 ml/1 tbsp vinegar in water
25-35 g/3-4 tbsp flour
2 eggs
Salt and pepper

▲ Scrape the earth, grit and black skins off the salsify. Cut into 1½-in/3.5-cm lengths and steep in acidulated water until you are ready to cook.
▲ Make a thin batter with the flour, eggs, salt and pepper. Cook the plain chopped salsify in boiling salted water for 10 minutes, then drain and pat dry with paper. Dip in the batter and fry in hot oil. Drain on paper towels and serve hot.

This is another traditional Irish potato dish. It is served in soup bowls in a mound with a well made in the middle for some melted butter.

Champ or Cally

Potato and Celeriac Purée

COOKING TIME: 20-30 MINUTES

INGREDIENTS

900 g/2 lb floury potatoes
1 celeriac
60 ml/4 tbsp butter
A little milk
Salt and pepper

▲ Peel the potatoes and celeriac. Cut into even-sized pieces and cook in salted water until tender. Drain and keep over a low heat for a few minutes to get rid of excess moisture.

▲ Mash very well with the butter and milk. Don't make it too sloppy. Season with salt and pepper. Brown a little under the grill (broiler) and serve with game or roast beef.

Champ or Cally

COOKING TIME: 20 MINUTES

INGREDIENTS

8 potatoes (new floury ones are best)
6 spring (green) onions
good 3/4 cup/200 ml7/fl oz milk
Pepper and salt
1/2 cup/100 g/1/4 lb butter
Fresh thyme

▲ Boil the potatoes until tender. Drain well and put them back over a very low heat, covering the pan with a clean tea towel (or dish cloth) to dry out the potatoes. Then mash the potatoes thoroughly.

▲ Chop the onions finely, using both the green and white parts. Place them in the milk and bring to the boil. Then pour the milk and onions onto the mashed potato and mash them in. Do not make it too sloppy. If this happens, dry out a little over a low heat.

▲ Add a little fresh thyme to the now creamy mash. Put in bowls with little wells of butter in the middle. Chopped chives are a nice garnish.

There are many versions of potato cakes in Ireland.

Sweet and Sour Red Cabbage

COOKING TIME: 1 HOUR OR MORE

INGREDIENTS

1 onion, sliced
Butter
1 red cabbage, shredded
1 large (tart) cooking apple, sliced
Approx 2½ cups/600 ml/1 pt vegetable or meat stock
Juniper berries
Cloves
15 ml/1 tbsp brown sugar
15 ml/1 tbsp red wine or cider

▲ Soften the onion slices in butter. Add the shredded cabbage and cook for a few minutes. Stir in the sliced apple, stock, berries and cloves to taste, and the other ingredients.
▲ Simmer for at least 1 hour, and longer, if desired. Red cabbage is not spoiled by long cooking.
▲ Serve with any game or pork dishes or Irish stew.

Potato Cakes 1

COOKING TIME: 25 MINUTES

INGREDIENTS

90 ml/6 tbsp butter
1½ cups/225 g/½ lb self-raising (rising) flour
Salt and pepper
225 g/½ lb freshly mashed potato
A little milk
Butter
Bacon

OVEN TEMPERATURE:
220°C/425°F/GAS MARK 7

▲ Preheat the oven. Rub the butter into the flour, together with a pinch of salt and pepper. Mix with the mashed potato and enough milk to make a soft dough.
▲ Roll out onto a floured board and cut into rounds or triangles. Place on a lightly oiled tray and bake for 25 minutes. Serve hot split with butter and bacon.

Potato Cakes 2

COOKING TIME: 20 MINUTES

INGREDIENTS

60 ml/4 tbsp butter
¾ cup/100 g/¼ lb flour
2.5 ml/½ tsp salt
2.5 ml/½ tsp baking powder
450 g/1 lb freshly mashed potatoes
Butter

▲ Rub the butter into the flour. Add the salt and baking powder and mix well. Pile in the potatoes and knead for a few minutes.
▲ Roll out onto a well-floured board with a floured rolling pin. Cook on a dry griddle until brown on both sides. Serve hot, dripping with butter.

INGREDIENTS

450 g/1 lb vegetables, such as potatoes, carrots, leeks, salsify, asparagus, peas and beans

Spring onions, finely chopped

Chives and radishes, finely chopped

1 hard-boiled egg, chopped

SALAD DRESSING

2 hard-boiled egg yolks

5 ml/1 tsp Dijon mustard or mustard powder

15 ml/1 tbsp wine vinegar or lemon juice

2/3 cup/150 ml/1/4 pt cream

Salt and pepper

Mixed Vegetable Salad with Irish Salad Dressing

PREPARATION TIME: 20 MINUTES

▲ Cut the vegetables into cubes or julienne strips. Cook until they are *al dente* (still crisp). Refresh in cold water to prevent over cooking.

▲ Make the dressing: pound the hard-boiled egg yolks with the mustard, then add the vinegar and mix to a paste. Add the cream in a thin stream. Season to taste and mix with the salad vegetables.

▲ Finally, sprinkle with the chopped spring onions, chives, radishes and hard-boiled egg.

This salad is very good with smoked salmon and with any herring dishes. It is also delicious on its own, accompanied with soda bread for a light lunch.

INGREDIENTS

675 g/1½ lb freshly boiled beetroot
Bunch of spring onions
Bunch of fresh dill, chopped
30 ml/2 tbsp chopped parsley
2 hard-boiled eggs, chopped
2 boiled potatoes, diced
Olive oil
Crushed garlic
Lemon juice

Michaelmas Salad

PREPARATION TIME: 10 MINUTES

▲ Put the first six ingredients in a glass bowl. Dress with a vinaigrette made with the olive oil, garlic and lemon juice. As a general rule combine in the following proportions – ⅓ lemon juice to ⅔ olive oil – and add garlic to taste.

Desserts, Breads and Baking

Whiskey Trifle 98

Irish Coffee Cake 100

Pears in Red Wine 101

Irish Coffee 101

Cranachan 102

Chocolate and Almond Sandwich 103

Walnut and Caramel Tarts 104

Queen of Puddings 105

Saffron Cake 108

Curd Cake 108

Apple and Oatmeal Cake 109

Boiled Orange and Almond Cake with Curd Cheese Icing 110

Seed Cake 111

Chocolate and Whiskey Cake 112

Christmas Cake 113

Brown Soda Bread 114

Irish Soda Bread 115

Oatcakes 115

Irish Coffee Pudding 116

Potato and Apple Cake 117

Barm Brack 119

Irish Tea Brack 119

Guinness Cake 119

Apple and Elderberry Tart 119

LEFT *Rich sheaves of wheat, golden in the Irish sun, await collection to be milled into flour to create Ireland's cornucopia of cakes and breads.*

Whiskey Trifle

INGREDIENTS

2 Swiss (jelly) rolls, or 450 g/1 lb sponge cake
Unsweetened preserved fruit, or a mixture of chopped fresh soft fruits (peaches, pears, berries, bananas, apricots, etc.)
2/3 cup/150 ml/1/4 pt whiskey
1 1/4 cups/300 ml/1/2 pt whipped cream
3 egg whites
Chopped almonds

FOR THE CUSTARD

1 egg
3 egg yolks
15 ml/1 tbsp granulated sugar
2 1/2 cups/600 ml/1 pt milk
1 vanilla pod

▲ Cut the swiss rolls into slices and drench them with whiskey. Line the bottom and sides of a glass bowl or soufflé dish with the swiss roll slices, then put a layer of fruit inside the sponge lining. Then make the custard.

▲ In a bowl, beat the egg and egg yolks together with the sugar. In a saucepan, scald the milk with the vanilla pod. Then strain the milk over the eggs and sugar, beating all the time.

▲ Cook the custard in the bowl over boiling water until it coats the back of a wooden spoon. Make sure the boiling water does not actually touch the custard, or you will end up with scrambled eggs.

▲ Pour the custard over the cake and fruit while hot. Leave to cool. Whip the cream and in another bowl whip the egg whites until stiff. Fold them into the whipped cream. Pile the white froth on top of the trifle and decorate with chopped walnuts.

A DROP OF THE HARD STUFF

It was Catholic monks who probably brought the art of distilling from the Continent to Ireland during the 5th and 6th centuries, but it was the Irish who developed and refined the skills of whiskey distillation. Today, the Bushmill's distilleries (top) are one of the only two now in operation, producing its own unique product (casked, above). The label (right) dates from the 1870s.

Irish Coffee Cake

PREPARATION AND COOKING TIME:
10 MINUTES + 40-50 MINUTES

INGREDIENTS

SPONGE

½ cup/100 g/4 oz butter

½ cup/100 g/4 oz castor sugar

2 eggs

⅔ cup/100 g/4 oz self-raising (rising) flour

30 ml/2 tbsp black coffee

SYRUP

⅔ cup/150 ml/¼ pt black coffee

¼ cup/50 g/2 oz castor sugar

15 ml/1 tbsp Irish whiskey

DECORATION

1⅓ cups/300 ml/½ pt double (heavy) cream

Glacé icing with whiskey

OVEN TEMPERATURE:
170°C/325°F/GAS MARK 3

▲ Preheat the oven. Cream the butter and sugar together until light and fluffy. Add the eggs one at a time, adding a little of the flour after each egg. Beat in the coffee and then fold in the rest of the flour.

▲ Divide the mixture in half and place in 8-in/20-cm sandwich tins and bake for about 40 minutes.

▲ To make the syrup, heat the coffee with the sugar until it melts, then add the whiskey. When the cake is almost cool, prick the underside with a fork and drip the syrup all over the cake. Fill the middle with whipped cream and whiskey.

▲ Make a glacé icing by adding a few drops of coffee to some sifted icing (confectioner's) sugar, then beating with a wooden spoon until it becomes glossy and can spread easily with a palette knife. Spread the icing on the top of the cake.

Pears in Red Wine

COOKING TIME: ABOUT 1 HOUR

INGREDIENTS

8 good-sized Conference (sweet) pears
Lemon juice and water
½ bottle red wine
60 ml/4 tbsp granulated sugar
1 vanilla pod
1 stick of cinnamon
15 ml/1 tbsp cornflour (cornstarch)

▲ Peel the pears carefully and place in acidulated water. Put the wine, sugar, vanilla pod and cinnamon in a pan and heat until dissolved.
▲ Poach the pears in the liquid until they are almost transparent. Drain the pears, reserve the liquid and blend it with cornflour.
▲ Cook the syrup again for a few minutes until thickened, then pour it over the pears and chill. Serve with pouring cream.

Irish Coffee

INGREDIENTS

30 ml/2 tbsp Irish whiskey
15 g/1 tsp brown sugar
175 ml/¼ pt strong coffee

TO SERVE:

45 ml/3 tbsp double (heavy) cream, lightly whipped

▲ Having warmed an Irish Coffee, or long, glass, add the sugar and whiskey and pour on the coffee. It is important to use a strong brew, so that the coffee complements the whiskey, rather than being drowned by it.
▲ To serve, pour the cream over and spoon onto the coffee and drink the warm liquid through the cool layer of cream.

Irish Coffee, the perfect end to an Irish meal.

Cranachan

PREPARATION TIME: 20 MINUTES

INGREDIENTS

1/3 cup/50 g/2 oz flaked almonds
2/3 cup/50 g/2 oz medium oatmeal
1 1/4 cup/300 ml/1/2 pt whipping, or double (heavy) cream
4 tbsp honey, to taste
60 ml/4 tbsp whiskey
15 ml/1 tbsp lemon juice
Raspberries

▲ Toast the almonds and oatmeal.

▲ Whip the cream in a bowl, and stir in the honey and whiskey. Fold in the almonds and oatmeal, and finally, the lemon juice. Serve in tall glasses garnished with raspberries.

Chocolate and Almond Sandwich

PREPARATION AND COOKING TIME:
20 MINUTES + COOLING

INGREDIENTS

½ cup/100 g/¼ lb butter
75 ml/5 tbsp granulated sugar
1 egg, beaten
90 ml/6 tbsp flour
90 ml/6 tbsp ground almonds
15 ml/1 tbsp cocoa
5 ml/1 tsp baking powder
1.25 ml/¼ tsp salt
45 ml/3 tbsp milk
Icing (confectioner's) sugar

CHOCOLATE FILLING

100 g/¼ lb grated chocolate
23 ml/1½ tbsp milk
bare 1 cup/150 g/5 oz icing (confectioner's) sugar
90 ml/6 tbsp unsalted (sweet) butter
Dash of almond essence (extract)

OVEN TEMPERATURE:
200°C/400°F/GAS MARK 6

▲ Preheat the oven. Cream the butter and sugar together. Add the well-beaten egg.

▲ In another bowl, sift together the flour, ground almonds, cocoa, baking powder and salt. Add alternately with the milk to the creamed butter and sugar. Combine thoroughly.

▲ Divide the mixture between two greased baking pans and bake for 20 minutes. When cool, sandwich together with the chocolate filling and dredge the top of the cake with icing (confectioner's) sugar.

▲ To make the filling, mix the chocolate with the milk and warm over a low heat until the chocolate has melted. Remove from the heat, beat in the icing sugar, then leave until cool.

▲ Cream the butter and then add the chocolate mixture and the almond essence (extract); beat until light and creamy. Fill the chocolate sandwich.

The quantities are for 8 tarts. It is usually advisable to make more, as they are so delicious they have a very short, sweet life.

INGREDIENTS

225 g/8 oz sweet flan pastry (see Pastry Making)

20 ml/1 generous tbsp honey

⅔ cup/150 ml/¼ pt double (heavy) cream

1½ cups/275 g/10 oz sugar

Pinch of cream of tartar

⅔ cup/150 ml/¼ pt water

1½ cups/175 g/6 oz walnut halves

OVEN TEMPERATURE: 200°C/400°F/GAS MARK 6

Walnut and Caramel Tarts

PREPARATION AND COOKING TIME: 30-40 MINUTES

▲ Preheat the oven. Make the pastry (*see* Pastry Making) and chill for about half an hour. Roll out the pastry and line the tartlet moulds and chill. Make sure the tart moulds have a high edge. Bake blind until the edges of the pastry begin to colour and cool on a wine rack.

▲ To make the filling, mix together the honey and the cream in a bowl. Put the sugar, cream of tartar and water in a deep, heavy-based saucepan and heat until dissolved. Raise the heat and boil to a light amber caramel.

▲ Stir the cream mixture into the caramel – stand back from the pan as it spatters. Boil without stirring until it reaches the soft boil stage – 115°C/239°F on a sugar thermometer. Be very careful handling this mixture, as it can cause severe burns.

▲ Turn the heat down and add the walnuts. Spoon the mixture into the tart shells and serve when cool.

INGREDIENTS

2½ cups/600 ml/1 pt milk and zest of 1 lemon

2 cups/100 g/4 oz fresh breadcrumbs

30 ml/2 tbsp sugar

60 ml/4 tbsp unsalted (sweet) butter

15 ml/1 tbsp Madeira

2 egg yolks

Jam (strawberry or raspberry)

4 egg whites and 225 g/½ lb granulated sugar

Whipped cream

OVEN TEMPERATURE: 180°C/350°F/GAS MARK 4

Queen of Puddings

PREPARATION AND COOKING TIME: 15 + 45 MINUTES

▲ Preheat the oven. Bring the milk to the boil on top of the stove with the lemon zest grated into it. Infuse for 5 minutes.

▲ Mix the breadcrumbs, butter and 30 ml/2 tbsp of sugar in a bowl. Strain on the milk, add a little Madeira, and leave for 10 minutes. Then add beaten egg yolks.

▲ Pour the mixture into a pie dish or Pyrex bowl and bake for about 20 minutes. Remove from the oven and spread the jam over the mixture.

▲ Whisk the egg whites until stiff and fold in the sugar to make a meringue mixture. Place on top of the jam in the dish or bowl and make peaks, using a fork.

▲ Put in the oven at 170°C/325°F/Gas mark 3 for 10 minutes. Then turn the oven down to 140°C/275°F/Gas mark 1 or less for 15 minutes.

▲ Serve hot with whipped cream.

ABOVE *Tourists and local inhabitants sampling the brew straight from the still. The illicit still (left) is hopefully concealed from the eyes of the local police.*

THE MYSTIQUE OF POTEEN

Illicit whiskey – called in Gaelic poteen – has been part of the Irish tradition ever since government taxation in the early 17th century forced production out of the home and into hiding. It is the father of all other illegal whiskies, notably American 'moonshine', which grew out of the distilling skills introduced by Irish immigrants.

Being illegal, poteen had to be made secretly – a task that tested Irish ingenuity to its fullest. Stills were hidden in caves, secret rooms, hollow stacks of peat, remote sea coves and on the banks of quiet streams – in fact, anywhere the distillers thought their activities would go undetected. The basic equipment required is a kettle to heat the mash – traditionally, this was malted barley, though other ingredients are now often substituted – the worm through which the resulting vapour is passed and a barrel to cool the vapour back to liquid. This is 'poteen', a strong, colourless spirit, with the raw kick of an unaged whiskey.

Curd cake is what is now known as cheesecake.

Saffron Cake

COOKING TIME: 45 MINUTES

INGREDIENTS

3 cups/450 g/1 lb flour
60 ml/4 tbsp granulated sugar
Good pinch of salt
½ cup/100g/¼ lb butter
Pinch of powdered mace
2.5 ml/½ tsp pounded cardamon seeds
⅔ cup/100 g/¼ lb raisins
½ cup/50 g/2 oz candied peel
30 ml/2 tbsp fresh yeast
⅔ cup/150 ml/¼ pt warm milk
Pinch of saffron

OVEN TEMPERATURE:
170°C/325°F/GAS MARK 3

▲ Preheat the oven. Sift the flour, sugar and salt and then rub in the butter. Mix in the mace, cardamon, raisins and the peel.
▲ Mix the yeast with the milk until it becomes frothy. Then stir in the saffron. Leave for a few minutes and beat into the dry mixture.
▲ Mix with your hand and leave in a warm place until it doubles in size. Turn onto a floured board and knead. Put into a round 8-in/20-cm pan and leave to rise again.
▲ Bake in a moderate oven for 45 minutes. Leave to cool on a rack.

Curd Cake

COOKING TIME: 30-35 MINUTES

INGREDIENTS

225 g/½ lb sweet flan pastry (see Basic Recipes)
2 eggs, separated
450 g/1 lb curd cheese or cottage cheese, pressed through a sieve (strainer)
60 ml/4 tbsp granulated sugar
60 ml/4 tbsp unsalted (sweet) butter
Juice and zest of 1 lemon

OVEN TEMPERATURE:
180°C/350°F/GAS MARK 4

▲ Preheat the oven. Make a sweet flan pastry and chill.
▲ Beat the egg yolks and mix with the curd cheese, sugar, softened butter, lemon juice and zest. Combine well. Then whisk the egg whites until stiff. Fold them into the curd cheese mixture.
▲ Roll out the pastry and line an 8-in/20-cm flan tin with a removable base. Bake blind until the edge of the pastry begins to colour. Then fill the pastry case and bake for 30-35 minutes.
▲ Serve warm with melted strawberry or raspberry jam brushed over the surface.

Apple and Oatmeal Cake

COOKING TIME: 30 MINUTES

INGREDIENTS

675 g/1½ lb peeled and sliced cooking (tart) apples
60 ml/4 tbsp brown sugar
5 ml/1 tsp cinnamon
⅓ cup/50 g/2 oz raisins

▲ Preheat the oven. Cook the apples, sugar and cinnamon in a saucepan until the apples form a pulp. Then add the raisins and cool.

▲ Melt the butter, sugar and honey in another saucepan. In a bowl, mix the oatmeal and lemon zest together, then pour into the honey mixture. Add the eggs and whiskey and mix well.

▲ Divide the oatmeal mixture into three. Put one layer of the oatmeal on the bottom of a greased cake tin. Cover with half the apple mixture. Top this with another layer of oatmeal. Then add the final apple layer, then finish off with the oatmeal.

▲ Bake for half an hour. Serve warm with cream.

FOR THE OATMEAL PASTRY:

½ cup/100 g/¼ lb unsalted (sweet) butter
20 ml/1 heaped tbsp brown sugar
30 ml/2 tbsp clear honey
zest of 1 lemon
3 cups/275 g/10 oz medium oatmeal
2 eggs, beaten
1 glass whiskey

OVEN TEMPERATURE:
190°C/375°F/GAS MARK 5

INGREDIENTS

2 oranges
2 cups/225 g/½ lb ground almonds
½ cup/100 g/¼ lb sugar
6 eggs
5 ml/1 tsp baking powder
Flour to dredge the pan

FOR THE ICING:

1 cup/175 g/6 oz curd cheese
½ cup/50 g/2 oz icing (confectioner's) sugar
30 ml/2 tbsp double (heavy) cream
15 ml/1 tbsp Grand Marnier, or Cointreau

OVEN TEMPERATURE:
190°C/375°F/GAS MARK 5

Boiled Orange and Almond Cake with Curd Cheese Icing

COOKING TIME: 2 HOURS

▲ Preheat the oven. Boil the oranges in their skins in water on top of the stove until they are very soft – this takes about an hour. Drain thoroughly.

▲ Beat the eggs and add the sugar, almonds and baking powder. Purée the chopped oranges in a food processor and add to the mixture. Oil and flour a 9-in/23-cm cake pan and pour in the mixture. Bake for about 1 hour. This is a very moist cake and may be served as a dessert, plain with cream, or with the curd cheese icing.

▲ To make the icing, put all the ingredients into a mixer or food processor. Blend. When they are well creamed spread on top of the cake.

Seed cake or 'seedy cake', as it was known in Dublin, was very popular with the ladies. It is traditionally washed down with a glass of port.

Seed Cake

COOKING TIME: 1½ HOURS

▲ Cream the butter and sugar. Beat in the eggs, one at a time, adding a little flour each time to prevent the mixture curdling.
▲ Fold in the rest of the flour and the caraway seeds. Stir in the milk and Kirsch.
▲ Bake in a round 8-in/20-cm baking dish, lined and greased, for about 1½ hours. Leave in the pan for a few minutes, then cool on a wire rack. This cake keeps for a long time in an airtight container.

INGREDIENTS

1 cup/225 g/ 8 oz butter
1 cup/225 g/½ lb granulated sugar
4 eggs
1½ cups/225 g/½ lb self-raising (rising) flour
20 ml/1 heaped tbsp caraway seeds
30 ml/2 tbsp milk
30 ml/2 tbsp Kirsch

OVEN TEMPERATURE:
170°C/325°F/GAS MARK 3

This recipe is from Marlfield House Restaurant in Co. Wexford.

Wexford has long been known as a centre of culinary excellence; the recipe for Chocolate and Whiskey Cake here comes from one of its best-known restaurants.

Chocolate and Whiskey Cake

PREPARATION TIME:
MINIMUM 4 HOURS, OR OVERNIGHT

INGREDIENTS

225 g/8 oz digestive biscuits
1 cup/225 g/8 oz dark cooking chocolate
225 g/½ lb butter
2 eggs
90 ml/6 tbsp granulated sugar
½ cup/100 g/4 oz glacé cherries
½ cup/50 g/2 oz walnuts
⅔ cup/150 ml/¼ pt Irish whiskey
75 ml/5 tbsp whipped cream

▲ Crush the biscuits coarsely and keep them aside.

▲ Melt the chocolate with the butter in a double boiler or saucepan. Cream the eggs and sugar in a bowl until they are pale and billowing, then fold in the chocolate.

▲ To this mixture add three-quarters of the cherries and the walnuts; save the rest for decoration. Fold in all but 15 ml/1 tbsp of whiskey.

▲ Oil a 9-in/23-cm baking dish, line with the crushed biscuits, then scrape all of the mixture into it. Decorate the top with the remaining cherries and walnuts and place in the refrigerator for several hours or overnight. Take it out of the fridge about half an hour before serving.

▲ Add the whiskey to the cream. Pipe around the top of the cake.

This recipe is from Monica Sheridan's column in the Irish Times. *She inherited it from her mother and I have been making it for years with great success.*
When it was first published in the Irish Times, *Monica received letters from all over the world. There is a street in Rome where all the inhabitants make it every Christmas.*

INGREDIENTS

- ¾ cup/175 g/6 oz glacé cherries
- 2 cups/350 g/¾ lb seedless raisins
- 2 cups/350 g/¾ lb sultanas (golden raisins)
- 1 cup/100 g/4 oz candied peel
- ½ cup/50 g/2 oz chopped angelica
- 1½ cups/175 g/6 oz chopped walnuts
- 350 g/¾ lb butter
- 350 g/¾ lb granulated sugar
- 7 eggs
- 2¼ cups/350 g/¾ lb flour
- 5 ml/1 tsp salt
- 5 ml/1 tsp mixed spice
- Irish whiskey

OVEN TEMPERATURE: BETWEEN 150°C/300°F/GAS MARK 2 AND 140°C/275°F/GAS MARK 1

Christmas Cake

PREPARATION AND COOKING TIME: SEVERAL HOURS OR 1 DAY + 6 HOURS

▲ Some hours (or a day) before making the cake, the following preparations are necessary. Preheat the oven to 140°C/275°F/Gas mark 1. Halve the cherries and put, together with the rest of the fruit and nuts, into a casserole. Mix them well together. Cover loosely with paper or foil and put into the warm oven until the fruit is well heated through.

▲ Toss the fruit and nuts once or twice to allow the heat to penetrate. This heating makes the fruit sticky and prevents it from sinking to the bottom of the cake. It also makes it plump and juicy. When all the fruit is heated through take it out of the oven and let it go cold.

▲ Cream the butter and sugar together until white and fluffy. Add the eggs, one at a time, with 5 ml/1 tsp of flour for each egg. This prevents the mixture from curdling.

▲ Sift the remaining flour with the salt and mixed spice. Fold into the egg mixture. Then fold in the fruit and nuts.

▲ Put the mixture into a high 10-in/25-cm greased cake pan that has been well lined with two thicknesses of greaseproof (waxed) paper. Flatten the mixture in the pan and make sure there is about 2 in/5 cm of pan above the mixture.

▲ Trim the lining paper level with the top of the pan and rest an inverted tin plate or lid over it.

▲ Put the cake in a low (150°C/300°F/Gas mark 2) oven for 1 hour, then reduce the heat to 140°C/275°F/Gas mark 1 for another 5 hours. The cake should be golden when ready. Do not remove it from the pan until it is cold. Then prick the bottom with a skewer and sprinkle liberally with Irish whiskey. This cake keeps for a long time in a tin.

Brown Soda Bread

PREPARATION AND COOKING TIME:
ABOUT 15 MINUTES + 40 MINUTES

Irish soda bread is arguably the best bread in the world. Many women in Ireland still make it every day. There is no waiting for it to rise nor does it involve endless kneading. The less soda bread is handled the better it will be. The following quantities will make two 675 g/1½ lb loaves. I have substituted yogurt and water for the traditionally used buttermilk.

INGREDIENTS

6 cups/900 g/2 lb wholemeal flour
3 cups/450 g/1 lb strong white flour
6 ml/1 heaped tsp bicarbonate of (baking soda)
70 ml/13 heaped tsp baking powder
Approx 2½ cups/600 ml1 pt natural yogurt mixed with water to the consistency of buttermilk
2 eggs
Good pinch of salt

OVEN TEMPERATURE: 190°C/375°F/GAS MARK 5, REDUCED TO 180°C/350°F/GAS MARK 4

▲ Preheat the oven. Place all the dry ingredients in a large mixing bowl. Combine well with the fingers.

▲ In another bowl mix the eggs with the yogurt and water.

▲ Make a well in the dry mixture and slowly pour on the yogurt and water. Mix with your hands until you get a nice soft dough – not too wet. A dough that is too wet or too stiff will result in a hard and heavy bread.

▲ Lightly flour a worktop or pastry board. Divide the dough in half. Make two flat rounds of bread on the board.

▲ Cut a deep cross in the middle of each loaf. Place in the preheated oven for 10 minutes, then reduce the heat. Bake until the bottom of the bread sounds hollow when knocked. This takes about half an hour.

Irish Soda Bread

INGREDIENTS

4 cups/450 g/1 lb plain white (all-purpose) flour
1 tsp salt
2 tsp bicarbonate of soda (baking soda)
1½ tsp cream of tartar
2 tbsp/25 g/1 oz lard
1¼ cups/300 ml/½ pt buttermilk

OVEN TEMPERATURE:
220°C/425°F/GAS MARK 7

MAKES 1 LOAF

▲ Sift the flour, salt, bicarbonate of soda and cream of tartar into a bowl. Rub in the lard and add enough buttermilk to make a soft dough. Turn the mixture on to a lightly floured board and knead for a minute. Shape into a round and place on the baking sheet. Mark with a cross, cutting deep into the dough.

▲ Bake for 40-50 minutes, until lightly browned and firm when tapped on the base. Cool the bread on a wire rack.

VARIATIONS: You can use plain milk instead of buttermilk, but if you do, double the quantity of cream of tartar. You can also use a mixture of white and wholewheat flours.

Oatcakes

COOKING TIME: ABOUT 20 MINUTES

INGREDIENTS

½ cup/100 g/4 oz medium oatmeal
Pinch of salt
Pinch of bicarbonate of soda
15 ml/1 tbsp melted bacon fat
Hot water

▲ Mix the dry ingredients in a bowl, make a well in the middle and pour in the melted fat. Add enough hot water to make a stiff paste.

▲ Scatter your work surface or board liberally with oatmeal and transfer the paste to the board, pressing with the hands. (Cover your hands with flour as the oatmeal is very sticky at this stage).

▲ Roll to about ¼ in/6 mm thickness and cut into 8-in/20-cm circles. Sprinkle with more oatmeal, then cut into quarters.

▲ Place on a hot griddle – a heavy frying pan will do – and cook until the edges curl a little. Then turn them over and cook on the other side, or finish them under a warm grill (broiler).

▲ They may also be baked in a moderate oven (180°C/350°F/Gas mark 4) for about 20 minutes.

This is another of Monica Sheridan's recipes.

Irish Coffee Pudding

PREPARATION TIME: ABOUT 1 HOUR

INGREDIENTS

6 eggs, separated
1 cup/225 g/½ lb sugar
1¼ cups/300 ml/½ pt very strong black coffee
40 g/1½ oz leaf gelatin(e)
110 ml/7 tbsp Irish whiskey
1¼ cups/300 ml/½ pt double (heavy) cream
90 ml/6 tbsp crushed walnuts (optional)
Whiskey-flavoured whipped cream (optional)

▲ In a bowl, cream the egg yolks with the sugar. Heat the coffee and dissolve the gelatin(e) in it. Then add it to the yolks and the sugar. Beat well.

▲ Put the bowl over a pan of boiling water and heat, stirring, until the mixture begins to thicken. Remove from the heat and, when the bowl has cooled a little, put it over cracked ice and continue to stir.

▲ When the mixture is on the point of setting, whip the cream and fold it in, together with the whiskey. Then fold in the stiffly beaten egg whites.

▲ Pour into individual glasses and leave to set. If desired, top with whiskey-flavoured whipped cream and crushed walnuts.

Instead of pastry, potato-cake dough is used for the crust. It is always baked on the top of the stove on a griddle or in a heavy iron pan. This is Monica Sheridan's version.

Potato and Apple Cake

COOKING TIME: ABOUT 30 MINUTES

INGREDIENTS

FOR THE POTATO CAKE MIXTURE:

60 ml/4 tbsp butter
¾ cup/100 g/¼ lb flour
2.5 ml/½ tsp salt
2.5 ml/½ tsp baking powder
450 g/1 lb freshly washed potatoes

FOR THE APPLE MIXTURE:

2 large cooking (tart) apples
A little sugar to taste
4-5 cloves
5 ml/1 tsp cinnamon
30 ml/2 tbsp butter

▲ Make a portion of potato-cake mixture (*see* Potato Cakes 2 for method). Divide the dough in two parts and roll out into two circles.

▲ Peel the apples and slice thinly. Put a few layers of them on one circle of dough. Cover with the other circle of dough and pinch the edges together. Cook gently on a greased pan, turning once to cook on the other side.

▲ When the apples are cooked through, lift back the top and sprinkle with sugar, cloves and cinnamon. Add a large pat of butter.

▲ Replace the top, leave on the heat for another 5 minutes, and eat very hot with cream or egg custard.

This version of brack (fruit bread) is made with baking powder, cold tea and whiskey.

Irish Tea Brack

Barm Brack

PREPARATION AND COOKING TIME:
1½ + 1 HOUR

INGREDIENTS

3 cups/450 g/1 lb flour
60 ml/4 tbsp butter
Grated nutmeg
Pinch of salt
20 g/¾ oz yeast
30 ml/2 tbsp sugar
2 eggs, beaten
1½ cups/225 g/½ lb sultanas
1½ cups/225 g/½ lb currants
1 cup/100 g/4 oz candied peel
1¼ cups/300 ml/½ pt milk

OVEN TEMPERATURE:
200°C/400°F/GAS MARK 6

▲ Preheat the oven. Sift the flour, nutmeg and salt together. Rub the butter into the flour.

▲ Cream the yeast in a cup with a tsp of the sugar. Add the rest of the sugar to the flour mixture and combine well. Scald the milk; add to the liquid yeast together with all but a little of the well-beaten eggs. Stir into the dry ingredients to produce a stiff but elastic batter. Fold in the fruit.

▲ Butter an 8-in/20-cm cake tin and pour in the dough. It should come halfway up the tin. Cover with a clean cloth and leave in a warm place to rise – it should double in size in about 1 hour.

▲ Brush the top of the brack with beaten egg to glaze. Bake until a skewer, or thin knife, comes out clean – about 1 hour.

Irish Tea Brack

PREPARATION TIME:
OVERNIGHT + 1 HOUR COOKING

INGREDIENTS

450 g/1 lb sultanas (golden raisins)
450 g/1 lb raisins
450 g/1 lb brown sugar
2 cups/450 ml/¾ pt black tea
2 cups/450 ml/¾ pt whiskey
450 g/1 lb flour
3 eggs, beaten
15 ml/1 tbsp baking powder
10 ml/2 tsp mixed spices

OVEN TEMPERATURE:
190°C/375°F/GAS MARK 5

▲ Soak the fruit with the sugar in the tea and whiskey overnight.

▲ Preheat the oven. Add the flour, eggs and the baking powder and spices to the fruit mixture.

▲ Mix all the ingredients together well and put in greased loaf tins.

▲ Bake for 1 hour. Allow to cool in the tin slightly before turning out to cool fully on a rack.

Guinness Cake

PREPARATION AND COOKING TIME:
OVERNIGHT + 2 HOURS

INGREDIENTS

½ cup/100 g/¼ lb butter
1 cup/225 g/8 oz brown sugar
3 eggs, beaten
2¼ cups/350 g/¾ lb self-raising (rising) flour
2.5 ml/½ tsp mixed spice
Pinch of salt
⅔ cup/100 g/4 oz raisins (soaked in Guinness overnight)
½ cup/50 g/2 oz candied peel (soaked)
1⅓ cups/225 g/8 oz sultanas (soaked)
¼ cup/50 g/2 oz glacé cherries
⅔ cup/150 ml/½ pt Guinness or dark beer

OVEN TEMPERATURE:
180°C/350°F/GAS MARK 4

▲ Preheat the oven. Cream the butter and sugar until the sugar is dissolved. Beat in the eggs.

▲ Add the flour, salt, mixed spice and the soaked dried fruit.

▲ Finally mix in the Guinness.

▲ Grease an 8-in/20-cm cake tin and pour the mixture in. Bake for about 2 hours.

Apple and Elderberry Tart

COOKING TIME: 30 MINUTES

INGREDIENTS

225 g/8 oz sweet flan pastry (see Pastry Making)
900 g/2 lb Cox's or other tart dessert apples
1¼ cups/300 ml/½ pt elderberries
Red currant jelly

OVEN TEMPERATURE:
200°C/400°F/GAS MARK 6

▲ Preheat the oven. Make the pastry, chill, then roll out and line a 10-in/25-cm flan tin.

▲ Core and cut the apples into eighths. Place them in the flan dish in concentric circles. Scatter the elderberries on top of the apples. Melt the redcurrant jelly and spread on top of the tart. Bake until the pastry is a golden brown. Serve with cream or with egg custard.

Basic Recipes

White or Poultry Stock 122

Brown Stock 122

Vegetable Stock 122

Fish Stock 122

Shortcrust Pastry 124

Sweet Tart Pastry 124

Flaky or Puff Pastry 124

Béchamel Sauce 125

Tomato Sauce 125

Hollandaise Sauce 125

Green Mayonnaise 125

LEFT *The Four Courts in Dublin, once a hated symbol of the British Ascendancy, but now restored to their former 18th-century glory.*

Stocks

There is no such thing as a good soup without a good stock. Like anything else in the Irish cooking tradition, stocks are extremely simple to make – it just takes a little care and decent ingredients. There are four basic types of stock which may be used for soups, sauces and casseroles. Stocks may also be reduced and frozen – a little stock-making session now and again can transform your cooking. Remember, nothing good ever comes out of a commercial stock cube.

White or Poultry Stock

COOKING TIME: 2 HOURS

INGREDIENTS

1 boiling fowl or poultry carcass (pork or veal bones may be used also)
2 large onions
1 leek
2 carrots
4 cloves of garlic
4 sticks and leaves of celery
1 large bunch of mixed fresh herbs – thyme, parsley, oregano and sage
6½ Am pt/3 L/5 pt water
1 dried bay leaf

▲ Put the chicken or bones in a large pot. Clean and peel all the vegetables but leave them whole and add, together with the water, to the pot. Tie the herbs in a bouquet and put it in the pot. Bring slowly to the boil and simmer for 2 hours.

▲ Skim any scum or froth off the top; strain the liquid off the vegetables as they will make the stock cloudy if they are left in. Leave in a cold place and take any oil or fat off the top.

▲ You now have a lovely clear stock, which may be reduced and concentrated by boiling very fast and frozen for future use.

Brown Stock

COOKING TIME: 1 HOUR 30 MINUTES

▲ Use beef, veal, mutton, ham or pork bones, or any combination of these. Ask your butcher or meat counter attendant to break up the bones. Clean and prepare the same vegetables as for white or poultry stock, with the addition of some white turnips.

▲ Put the bones in a hot oven to brown, basting now and again. After about half an hour, take them out, drain off any fat and put them in a large saucepan. Brown the vegetables in the fat and add them to the bones.

▲ Cover with 6½ Am pt/3 L/5 pt of water and add the bunch of herbs and continue as for the white stock.

Vegetable Stock

COOKING TIME: 30 MINUTES

INGREDIENTS

900 g/2 lb potato
30 ml/2 tbsp olive oil
2 large onions, roughly chopped
10 cloves of garlic
1 leek, chopped
2 sticks of celery, chopped
2 carrots, roughly chopped
2 turnips, roughly chopped
A few fresh or dried mushrooms
4 soft tomatoes
Large bunch of herbs
3¾ Am pt/1.7 L/3 pt water

There is no need for vegetarian soups to be insipid, watery affairs. A potato-peel stock or broth gives a good base to any vegetable soup or stew. Note: you will notice that I have not added salt or pepper to the stocks. Adding salt is dangerous, as the stock may be greatly reduced and become too salty to use – it is better to wait and season the final dish.

▲ Scrub and peel the potatoes. Put only the peelings in a large pot with the oil – add all the other roughly chopped vegetables. Brown them a little, then add the water and the herbs and simmer for 30 minutes.

▲ Strain and use for soups, sauces and stews.

Fish Stock

COOKING TIME: 20 MINUTES

Fish stock is so quick to make that it is not really worth bothering to freeze it. Use any white fish bones and heads – avoid oily fish as it becomes too strong and has a rather unpleasant taste, reminiscent of cod liver oil. Salmon may be used for salmon dishes but otherwise this also is too oily.

INGREDIENTS

450 g/1 lb fish heads, trimmings and bones
2 onions, sliced
60 ml/4 tbsp unsalted (sweet) butter
4 cloves of garlic
1 head of fennel, if available, sliced
Bunch of parsley, chopped
2 bay leaves, torn
1 piece of lemon peel
Lemon juice
5 cups/1.1 L/2 pt mixed white wine and water

▲ Soften the onions in a little unsalted butter. Add the other ingredients and cover with the water and the wine. Simmer for about 20 minutes. Strain and cool.

▲ A shellfish stock may be made with shellfish trimmings or shells and a few mussels.

Cows being driven home from the fields for evening milking and grazing peacefully in rich pasture – a traditional Irish scene that has barely changed over the centuries.

Shortcrust Pastry

PREPARATION TIME:
10 MINUTES + 30 MINUTES

INGREDIENTS

1⅓ cups/225 g/½ lb plain (all-purpose) flour

Pinch of salt

½ cup/100 g/4 oz unsalted butter

1 egg yolk

Iced water

▲ Put the flour and salt in a bowl. Cut the butter into small pieces and blend into the flour with your fingers until the mixture resembles breadcrumbs.

▲ Make a well in the middle and add the egg yolk, then mix in some cold water – enough to make a firm dough.

▲ Rest the mixture in the refrigerator for about 30 minutes, then use as required.

▲ Bake at 200°C/400°F/Gas mark 6 until golden.

Sweet Tart Pastry

INGREDIENTS

1⅓ cups/200 g/7 oz flour

75 ml/5 tbsp sugar

Pinch of salt

90 ml/6 tbsp unsalted (sweet) butter

3 egg yolks

Vanilla essence (extract) to taste

▲ Mix all the dry ingredients together. Chop the butter and blend into the flour mixture with the fingers until it looks like fine breadcrumbs.

▲ Mix in the egg yolks and vanilla essence (extract) until you have a firm pastry. Chill for 30 minutes before rolling out.

Flaky or Puff Pastry

PREPARATION TIME: 1 HOUR

INGREDIENTS

2¼ cups/350 g/¾ lb plain (all-purpose) flour

Good pinch of salt

1 cup/225 g/½ lb unsalted (sweet) butter, cut into small pieces

⅔ cup/150 ml/¼ pt ice-cold water

▲ Sift the flour and salt into a large basin or bowl. Rub in ½ cup/100 g/¼ lb of the butter with the fingers, then add the water and combine to form a stiff mixture. Rest for about 20 minutes in the refrigerator.

▲ Roll out the pastry and spread the rest of the butter over one third. Fold the pastry over to cover the butter and roll out again gently, making sure the butter does not come through the pastry. If this happens you will have a very oily rather than a crisp, flaky pastry.

▲ Fold the pastry into three. Rest it for 5 minutes and roll out again. Finally, roll the pastry out until ⅛ in/3 mm thick and use for sweet or savoury pies.

▲ When ready to use, cook at 200°C/400°F/Gas mark 6 until well-risen and golden brown.

Béchamel Sauce

COOKING TIME: 45 MINUTES
TO MAKE 2½ CUPS/600 ML/1 PT OF SAUCE

INGREDIENTS

30 ml/2 tbsp unsalted (sweet) butter
60 ml/4 tbsp flour
2½ cups/600 ml/1 pt milk
2 bay leaves
Sprig of fresh thyme
1 onion
Freshly grated nutmeg
Salt and pepper to taste

▲ Prepare a roux: melt the butter in a pan and mix in the flour over a low heat. Allow the roux to cook but not brown. Gradually add the milk, stirring or whisking continuously to prevent lumps forming.

▲ Bring the sauce to the boil, stirring, add the herbs and onion and simmer for at least 30 minutes. Take care that the sauce does not burn or stick to the pan.

▲ When the sauce is ready, strain it and add the freshly grated nutmeg and seasoning.

▲ *Variations:* Add some well-flavoured, hard, grated cheese to taste for a rich cheese sauce.

▲ For a parsley sauce, add a handful of chopped parsley and a little softened onion.

Tomato Sauce

COOKING TIME: 1 HOUR
TO MAKE 2½ CUPS/600 ML/1 PT OF SAUCE

INGREDIENTS

60 ml/4 tbsp olive oil or bacon fat
2 large onions, chopped
6 large cloves of garlic, crushed
900 g/2 lb ripe tomatoes, peeled, seeded and chopped, or 2 cans of chopped tomatoes
Bouquet garni
Salt and freshly ground black pepper
15 ml/1 tbsp tomato purée
15 ml/1 tbsp chopped basil, if available, or parsley

▲ Heat the oil or fat in a pan and cook the onions and garlic for about 15 minutes. Add the tomatoes, bouquet garni and seasoning and bring to the boil.

▲ Add the tomato purée, stir well and simmer for 45 minutes. Remove the pan from the heat, adjust the seasoning and add some chopped fresh basil, if in season, or parsley.

Hollandaise Sauce

MAKES 1⅓ CUPS/300 ML/½ P

INGREDIENTS

¾ cup/160 g/6 oz unsalted (sweet) butter
3 egg yolks
45 ml/3 tbsp water
Salt
Juice of half a lemon

▲ Melt the butter and let it cool a little. Remove any white scum from the surface.

▲ In a small, heavy-bottomed saucepan whisk the egg yolks with the water. Over a very low heat whisk until the mixture is thick and creamy. On no account let the mixture get too hot.

▲ Take the pan off the heat and whisk in the butter, drop by drop. When it begins to thicken add the butter a little faster.

▲ Add the salt and lemon juice to taste.

Green Mayonnaise

PREPARATION TIME: ABOUT 15 MINUTES

INGREDIENTS

2 egg yolks
Lemon juice
2½ cups/600 ml/1 pt sunflower oil
15 ml/1 tbsp mixed fresh herbs (basil, parsley, sorrel, coriander, chives)
1 clove of garlic
Salt

▲ Place the egg yolks in a mixer or blender with some lemon juice. Set the machine at a moderate speed and at first gently drip the oil in. When it begins to emulsify, pour in a steady stream until the oil is used up.

▲ Pound the herbs with the garlic and salt in a pestle and mortar, then mix these in with the mayonnaise.

▲ This mayonnaise may be kept in a sealed container in the refrigerator.

Index

Note: Page numbers in italics refer to captions of illustrations; numbers in bold type indicate information that is not part of a recipe.

A

almonds
Boiled Orange and Almond Cake with Curd Cheese Icing 110
Chocolate and Almond Sandwich 103
Cranachan 102
Angels on Horseback 43
apples
Apple and Elderberry Tart 119
Apple and Oatmeal Cake 109
Apple Purée 26
Braised Pheasant with Apple and Cream Sauce 82
Chicken, Apple and Black Pudding Filling 30
Michaelmas Goose with Red Cabbage, Apple and Chestnuts 77
Potato and Apple Cake 117
Roast Stuffed Pork Steak 72
Stuffed Apples 81

B

bacon
Angels on Horseback 43
Cod Baked with Bacon 45
Dublin Coddle 70
Game Pie 80
Hare Pudding 83
Pigeon and Bacon Pie with Stuffed Apples 81
Poached Turkey with Celery Sauce 76
Stuffed Onions 90
Sweetbreads with Bacon 30
Baked Stuffed Salmon with Cucumber Sauce 35
Baked Stuffed Trout 37
Ballybunion *38*
Bantry Bay, Cork *49*
barley
Mutton Broth with Barley 11
Barm Brack 119
Basic Recipes 121-5
batter recipes
Buttermilk Pancakes 30
Fried Oysters 42
Salsify Fritters 90
beans, haricot
Mutton Broth with Barley 11
Béarnaise sauce
Roast Ribs of Beef with Béarnaise Sauce 58
Béchamel Sauce 125
Fish Creams 27
Kedgeree 54
Smoked Fish Pie 46
Soft-Boiled Eggs in Ramekins with Onion Sauce 24
Sorrel-Stuffed Turnips 88
Spinach and Chopped Egg Filling 31
Stuffed Onions 90
beef
Beef in Guinness 61
Beef Stew with Herb Dumplings 66
Gaelic Steak 59
Irish Spiced Beef 62
Roast Ribs of Beef with Béarnaise Sauce 58
Salt Beef with Cabbage and Parsley Sauce 63
Wellington Beef 60
beer, brown
Irish Spiced Beef 62
beetroot
Michaelmas Salad 95
black pudding
Black Pudding with Apple Purée 26
Chicken, Apple and Black Pudding Filling 30
Bocuse, Paul: on Irish Stew **68**
Boiled Orange and Almond Cake with Curd Cheese Icing 110
Boxty on the Griddle 89
brack (fruit breads)
Barm Brack 119
Irish Tea Brack 119
Braised Ham with Prunes 71
Braised Pheasant with Apple and Cream Sauce 82
bread *see also* brack
Brown Soda Bread 114
Irish Soda Bread 115
bread, in recipes
croutons 15, 19;
fried bread, toast 24, 29, 30, 40
Queen of Puddings 105
Brotchan Roy 11
Brown Stock 122
Bushmill's Distilleries *99*
butter
herb, garlic butter **34**
Dublin Bay Prawns in Garlic Butter 51
Griddled Salmon Steaks with Herb Butter 34
Buttermilk Pancakes 30
fillings 30, 31

C

cabbage
Colcannon 88
Michaelmas Goose with Red Cabbage, Apple and Chestnuts 77
Salt Beef with Cabbage and Parsley Sauce 63
Sweet and Sour Red Cabbage 93
cakes
in trifle 98
Apple and Oatmeal Cake 109
Boiled Orange and Almond Cake with Curd Cheese Icing 110
Chocolate and Almond Sandwich 103
Chocolate and Whiskey Cake 112
Christmas Cake 113
Guinness Cake 119
Irish Coffee Cake 100
Potato and Apple Cake 117
Saffron Cake 108
Seed Cake 111
Cally (Champ) 91
capers
Mutton in Caper Sauce **11,** 69
Ray with Brown Butter Sauce 48
caraway seeds
Seed Cake 111
caramel
Walnut and Caramel Tarts 104
carrageen 86, **86**
carrots
Mutton in Caper Sauce 69
Cashel Cheese and Celery Soup 15
celeriac
Potato and Celeriac Purée 91
celery
Cashel Cheese and Celery Soup 15
Poached Turkey with Celery Sauce 76
Champ (Cally) 91
Champagne
Oysters in Champagne Sauce 42
Scallops in Champagne Sauce 38
cheese
Boiled Orange and Almond Cake with Curd Cheese Icing 110
Cashel Cheese and Celery Soup 15
Curd Cake (Cheesecake) 108
Fish Creams 27
chestnuts
Michaelmas Goose with Red Cabbage, Apple and Chestnuts 77
chicken
Chicken and Mushroom Pie 78
Chicken, Apple and Black Pudding Filling 30
chicken livers
Chicken Livers with Marsala 24
Game Pie 80
Chocolate and Almond Sandwich 103
Chocolate and Whiskey Cake 112
Christmas Cake 113
cider
Braised Ham with Prunes 71
Braised Pheasant with Apple and Cream Sauce 82
Dublin Coddle 70
clementines, spiced **79**
cod
Cod Baked with Bacon 45
Kedgeree 54
coffee
Irish Coffee 101
Irish Coffee Cake 100
Irish Coffee Pudding 116
Colcannon 88
County Cork 57
Bantry Bay *49*
crab
preparing crab 52
Creamed Crab 53
Devilled Crab 53
Cranachan 102
cream
Braised Pheasant with Apple and Cream Sauce 82
Cranachan 102
Irish Coffee 101
Irish Coffee Cake 100
Irish Coffee Pudding 116
Walnut and Caramel Tarts 104
Whiskey Trifle 98
cream, soured
Soused Herring with Sour Cream 55
Creamed Crab 53
croutons: with soups 15, 19
crystal: Waterford Crystal *64-5*
cucumber
Baked Stuffed Salmon with Cucumber Sauce 35
Curd Cake 108

D

desserts, bread and baking 96-119
Devilled Crab 53
dill
Michaelmas Salad 95
dillisk (dulse) 86, **86**
Dublin, Four Courts *120*
Dublin Bay Prawns in Garlic Butter 51
Dublin Coddle 70
Dublin Lawyer 50
duck *74*
Wild Duck **79**
Wild Duck with Spiced Oranges 79
dulse (dillisk) 86, **86**
dumplings
Beef Stew with Herb Dumplings 66

E

egg noodles
  Seaweed Salad 87
eggs
  Chicken Livers with Marsala 24
  Kedgeree 54
  Michaelmas Salad 95
  Scrambled Eggs with Smoked Salmon 29
  Soft-Boiled Eggs in Ramekins with Onion Sauce 24
  Spinach and Chopped Egg Filling 31
  Wicklow Pancakes 23
  Wild Mushroom Omelette 22
elderberries
  Apple and Elderberry Tart 119

F

fennel
  Sea Bass Cooked with Seaweed in a Paper Case 47
finan haddie
  Smoked Fish Pie 46
fish and shellfish **17**, *28*, **34**, 32-55
  Fish Creams 27
  Fish Soup 18
  Fish Steaks with Mussels 45
  Fish Stock 122
  Smoked Fish Pie 46
Fitzgibbon, Theodora
  White Onion Soup 13
Flaky Pastry 124
Flounder (Plaice) with Mustard Sauce 48
Fried Oysters 42
fritters
  Salsify Fritters 90
fruit breads
  Barm Brack 119
  Irish Tea Brack 119
fruit cakes
  Christmas Cake 113
  Guinness Cake 119

G

Gaelic Steak 59
Galway, oysters **43**
game 79-83
  Game Pie 80
garlic butter 34
  Dublin Bay Prawns with Garlic Butter 51
gelatine, carrageen as alternative **86**
Giant's Causeway, County Antrim *86*
goose 77
  Michaelmas Goose with Red Cabbage, Apple and Chestnuts 77
Green Mayonnaise 125
  Creamed Crab 53
Griddled Salmon Steaks with Herb Butter 34
Guinness *61*
  Beef in Guinness 61
  Guinness Cake 119
  Irish Spiced Beef 62

H

haddock, smoked
  Fish Creams 27
  Kedgeree 54
  Smoked Fish Pie 46
ham
  Braised Ham with Prunes 71
  Game Pie 80
  Ham with Onion and Parsley Sauce Filling **31**
  Pea and Ham Soup 12
  Stuffed Onions 90
hare, coursing *82*
  Hare Pudding 83
herb butters **34**
herb dumplings 66
herrings **95**
  Soused Herrings with Sour Cream 55
Hollandaise Sauce 125
  Oysters in Champagne Sauce 42
honey
  Cranachan 102
  Walnut and Caramel Tarts 104

I

Irish Coffee 101
Irish Coffee Cake 100
Irish Coffee Pudding 116
Irish moss (Carrageen) 86, **86**
Irish Soda Bread 115
Irish Spiced Beef 62
Irish Stew 68
Irish Tea Brack 119

K

kale
  Colcannon 88
Kedgeree 54
kidneys: Pork Ciste 73
Kilkenny *73*
Killybegs Harbour **46**

L

lamb, herb butters **34**
  Rack of Lamb in a Mustard Crust with Mint Sauce or Jelly 67
leeks
  Brotchan Roy 11
  Leek and Mussel Soup 17
  Leek and Potato Soup 19
lobster
  Dublin Lawyer 50

M

Marlfield House Restaurant, County Wexford *112*
Marsala
  Chicken Livers with Marsala 24
Mayonnaise, Green 125
  Creamed Crab 53
meat dishes 57-73
Michaelmas Goose with Red Cabbage, Apple and Chestnuts 77
Michaelmas Salad 95
Mixed Vegetable Salad with Irish Salad Dressing 94
mushrooms, wild **22**
  Chicken and Mushroom Pie 78
  Fish Creams 27
  Game Pie 80
  Pigeon and Bacon Pie with Stuffed Apples 81
  Scallops Served on the Shell with Mushrooms and Duchesse Potatoes 39
  Wellington Beef 60
  Wild Mushroom Omelette 22
mussels
  Fish Steaks with Mussels 45
  Leek and Mussel Soup 17
  Mussel and Onion Stew 40
  Stuffed Mussels 41
mustard
  Plaice (Flounder) with Mustard Sauce 48
  Rack of Lamb in a Mustard Crust with Mint Sauce or Jelly 67
mutton *11*, **11**, **69**
  Mutton Broth with Barley 11
  Mutton in Caper Sauce 69

N

noodles, egg
  Seaweed Salad 87

O

oatmeal
  Apple and Oatmeal Cake 109
  Brotchan Roy 11
  Cranachan 102
  Oatcakes **11**, 115
  Sorrel Soup 15
omelette
  Wild Mushroom Omelette 22
onions **31**
  Boxty on the Griddle 89
  Fish Creams 27
  Irish Stew 68
  Mussel and Onion Stew 40
  Mutton in Caper Sauce 69
  Soft-Boiled Eggs in Ramekins with Onion Sauce 24
  Stuffed Onions 90
  White Onion Soup 13
  Wicklow Pancakes 23
onions, spring
  Champ (Cally) 91
  Colcannon 88
  Michaelmas Salad 95
oranges
  Boiled Orange and Almond Cake with Curd Cheese Icing 110
  Wild Duck with Spiced Oranges 79
oysters *43*, **43**
  Angels on Horseback 43
  Beef in Guinness 61
  Fried Oysters 42
  Oysters in Champagne Sauce 42

P

pancakes
  Boxty on the Griddle 89
  Buttermilk Pancakes 30
    fillings 30, 31
  Wicklow Pancakes 23
parsley
  Brotchan Roy 11
  Fish Creams 27
  Ham with Onion and Parsley Sauce Filling **31**
  Michaelmas Salad 95
  Salt Beef with Cabbage and Parsley Sauce 63
parsnips
  Boxty on the Griddle 89
partridge
  Game Pie 80
pastry
  Flaky (Puff) Pastry 124
  Shortcrust Pastry 124
  Sweet Tart Pastry 124
pastry dishes (savoury)
  Chicken and Mushroom Pie 78
  Game Pie 80
  Hare Pudding (suet pastry) 83
  Pigeon and Bacon Pie with Stuffed Apples 81
  Pork Ciste (suet pastry) 73
  Smoked Fish Pie 46
  Wellington Beef 60
pastry dishes (sweet)
  Apple and Elderberry Tart 119
  Apple and Oatmeal Cake 109
  Curd Cake (Cheesecake) 108
  Walnut and Caramel Tarts 104
Pears in Red Wine 101
peas, dried **12**
  Pea and Ham Soup 12

pheasant
Braised Pheasant with Apple and Cream sauce 82
Game Pie 80
pies *see* pastry dishes (savoury)
pigeon
Game Pie 80
Pigeon and Bacon Pie with Stuffed Apples 81
Plaice (Flounder) with Mustard Sauce 48
Poached Salmon with Sorrel Sauce 36
Poached Turkey with Celery Sauce 76
pork
Game Pie 80
Port Ciste 73
pork steak **72**
Roast Stuffed Pork Steak 72
pork sausages
Dublin Coddle 70
Portrush *33*
potatoes *93*
Boxty on the Griddle 89
Champ (Cally) 91
Cod Baked with Bacon 45
Colcannon 88
Irish Stew 68
Leek and Potato Soup 19
Michaelmas Goose with Red Cabbage, Apple and Chestnuts 77
Michaelmas Salad 95
Potato and Apple Cake 117
Potato and Celeriac Purée 91
potato cakes **45**
Potato Cakes (2 recipes) 93
Roast Stuffed Pork Steak 72
Scallops Served on the Shell with Mushrooms and Duchesse Potatoes 39
Vegetable Stock (potato peelings) 122
Wicklow Pancakes 23
poteen *106, 107*
poultry and game 74-83
Poultry Stock 122
Powerscourt, County Wicklow *22*
prawns
Dublin Bay Prawns in Garlic Butter 51
Smoked Fish Pie 46
prunes
Braised Ham with Prunes 71
puddings (savoury, suet)
Hare, Pudding 83
Pork Ciste 73
puddings (sweet)
Apple and Oatmeal Cake 109
Irish Coffee Pudding 116
Potato and Apple Cake 117
Queen of Puddings 105
Puff Pastry 124

Q

Queen of Puddings 105

R

Rack of Lamb in a Mustard Crust with Mint Sauce or Jelly 67
Ray with Brown Butter Sauce 48
rice
Fish Steaks with Mussels 45
Kedgeree 54
Sweetbreads with Bacon **30**
Roast Ribs of Beef with Béarnaise Sauce 58
Roast Stuffed Pork Steak 72
Rock of Cashel, Tipperary *15*

S

Saffron Cake 108
salads
Michaelmas Salad 95
Mixed Vegetable Salad with Irish Salad Dressing 94
Seaweed Salad 87
salad dressings 94, 95
salmon *28,* **95, 122**
Baked Stuffed Salmon with Cucumber Sauce 35
Griddled Salmon Steaks with Herb Butter 34
Poached Salmon with Sorrel Sauce 36
Scrambled Eggs with Smoked Salmon 29
Smoked Salmon Stuffed Tomatoes 28
Salsify Fritters 90
Salt Beef with Cabbage and Parsley Sauce 63
sauces
apple and cream 82
Béarnaise 58
Béchamel 125
cheese 125
parsley 125
brown butter 48
caper 69
celery 76
Champagne 38, 42
cucumber 35
Hollandaise Sauce 125
mustard 48
onion 24
sorrel 36
Tomato Sauce 125
sausages
Dublin Coddle 70
Scallops in Champagne Sauce 38
Scallops Served on the Shell with Mushrooms and Duchesse Potatoes 39
Scrambled Eggs with Smoked Salmon 29
Sea Bass Cooked with Seaweed in a Paper Case 47
seaweed **43, 46,** 47, *47,* 86, **86**
Seaweed Salad 87
Seed Cake 111
Sheridan, Monica 113, 116
Shortcrust Pastry 124
silverside
Salt Beef with Cabbage and Parsley Sauce 63
sloke 86, **86**
Smoked Fish Pie 46
Smoked Salmon Stuffed Tomatoes 28
soda bread
Brown Soda Bread 114
Irish Soda Bread 115
Soft-Boiled Eggs in Ramekins with Onion Sauce 24
sorrel
Poached Salmon with Sorrel Sauce 36
Sorrel Soup 15
Sorrel-Stuffed Turnips 88
soups 8-19
Brotchan Roy 11
Cashel Cheese and Celery Soup 15
Fish Soup 18
Leek and Mussel Soup 17
Leek and Potato Soup 19
Mutton Broth with Barley 11
Pea and Ham Soup 12
Sorrel Soup 15
stocks 122
White Onion Soup 13
Soused Herrings with Sour Cream 55
Spinach and Chopped Egg Filling 31
starters and egg dishes 20-31
steak *see* beef
stews: stocks 122; with dulse **86**
Beef Stew with Herb Dumplings 66
Irish Stew 68
Mussel and Onion Stew 40
stocks 122
Stuffed Apples 81
Stuffed Mussels 41
Stuffed Onions 90
suet pastry dishes
Hare Pudding 83
Pork Ciste 73
Sweet and Sour Red Cabbage 93
Sweet Tart Pastry 124
Sweetbreads with Bacon 30

T

tarts
Apple and Elderberry Tart 119
Walnut and Caramel Tarts 104
toast: in recipes 24, 29, 30
tomatoes
Fish Steaks with Mussels 45
Smoked Salmon Stuffed Tomatoes 28
Tomato Sauce 125
Tralee Bay, County Kerry *43*
trifle
Whiskey Trifle 98
trout *28*
Baked Stuffed Trout 37
turkey
Poached Turkey with Celery Sauce 76
turnips
Mutton in Caper Sauce 69
Sorrel-Stuffed Turnips 88

V

veal
Game Pie 80
vegetables (and salads) 84-95
vegetables, mixed
Beef Stew with Herb Dumplings 66
Dublin Coddle 70
Fish Soup 18
Mixed Vegetable Salad with Irish Salad Dressing 94
Mussel and Onion Stew 40
Mutton Broth with Barley 11
Vegetable Stock 122
venison
Game Pie 80

W

Walnut and Caramel Tarts 104
Waterford Crystal *64-5*
Wellington Beef 60
Wexford County, Marlfield House Restaurant 112
whiskey, Irish *59, 99;* illicit (poteen) *106, 107*
Chocolate and Whiskey Cake 112
Cranachan 102
Dublin Lawyer 50
Irish Coffee 101
Irish Coffee Cake 100
Irish Coffee Pudding 116
Irish Tea Brack 119
Whiskey Trifle 98
White Onion Soup 13
White Stock 122
Wicklow Pancakes 23
Wild Duck with Spiced Oranges 79
Wild Mushroom Omelette 22
wine
Leek and Mussel Soup 17
Pears in Red Wine 101